CROCKPOT KETO

50 + Low-carb Recipes for Your Ketogenic Diet

(Easy and Delicious Crock Pot Recipes With Meal Plan for Busy People)

Ryan Krueger

Published by Alex Howard
© **Ryan Krueger**

All Rights Reserved

Crockpot Keto: 50 + Low-carb Recipes for Your Ketogenic Diet (Easy and Delicious Crock Pot Recipes With Meal Plan for Busy People)

ISBN 978-1-990169-95-3

All rights reserved. No part of this guide may be reproduced in any form without permission in writing from the publisher except in the case of brief quotations embodied in critical articles or reviews.

Legal & Disclaimer

The information contained in this book is not designed to replace or take the place of any form of medicine or professional medical advice. The information in this book has been provided for educational and entertainment purposes only.

The information contained in this book has been compiled from sources deemed reliable, and it is accurate to the best of the Author's knowledge; however, the Author cannot guarantee its accuracy and validity and cannot be held liable for any errors or omissions. Changes are periodically made to this book. You must consult your doctor or get professional medical advice before using any of the suggested remedies, techniques, or information in this book.

Table of contents

Part 1 1
Introduction 2
Chapter 1: Crock-pot Soup Recipes 3
Lentil Soup: 3
½ cup freshly chopped chives 3
Turkey, Kale and Cauliflower Soup 5
1 tablespoon coconut oil for greasing the pot 5
Potato and Corn Chowder 6
1 tablespoon unsalted butter 6
Baked Potato Soup 7
Cheeseburger Soup 8
Irish Beef Soup 10
Savory Cheese Soup 11
BBQ Chicken Soup 12
Mexican Chicken Soup: 13
Creamy Tomato Soup 15
Chapter 2: Crock-pot Chicken Recipes 17
Roast Chicken & Potatoes: 17
1 tablespoon lemon juice for garnishing 17
Crock-pot Chicken: 19
Sesame – Ginger Chicken: 20
Creamy Chicken and Mushroom Potpie 22
Hawaiian Chicken 24
Chicken Paprikash 25
Chapter 3: Crock-pot Turkey Recipes 26

Turkey Osso Buco	26
Turkey Madeira	28
Turkey Pad Thai	29
Hearty Jambalaya	31
Turkey Stew with Roasted Hatch chilies	33
Mediterranean Roast Turkey	35
Chapter 4: Crock-pot Beef Recipes	36
Korean Beef	36
Slow cooked Spaghetti Sauce	38
Salisbury steak	40
Beef Nachos	42
Italian Beef:	44
Autumn Pot Roast	45
Chapter 5: Crock-pot Pork Recipes	47
Spaghetti squash and Meatballs	47
Mexican Posole	48
Portuguese Chorizo and Peppers	50
Honey Soy Pork Tenderloin	51
Szechuan Pork	52
Chapter 6: Crock-pot Lamb Recipes	54
Braised Lamb Shanks	54
Slow cooked leg of lamb:	56
Moroccan Lamb	57
Irish Lamb Stew	59
Slow cooked Lamb Roast with Root Vegetables	60
Smoky Spiced Lamb Chops	62
Chapter 7: Crock-pot Seafood Recipes	63

Slow cooker Thai Green Fish Curry 63

Low country Boil 65

Shrimp Arrabbiata 67

Seafood Stew 68

Lemony Shrimp Risotto 70

Seafood Gumbo: 72

Chapter 8: Crock-pot Vegetarian Recipes 74

Mixed Vegetable Curry: 74

Cauliflower Bolognese with Zucchini Noodles 76

Chinese Tofu and Vegetables 78

Enchilada Quinoa 80

Mediterranean Stew: 81

Vegetarian Chili: 82

Conclusion 84

Part 2 85

Introduction 86

Meat 87

BBQ Beef BrisketServing: 6-8 87

Red Beans and SausageServing: 10 88

Beef Tips in GravyServings: 6 89

Beef EnchiladasServings: 12 91

Stuffed MeatballsServings: 4-6 93

Taco LasagnaServings: 6 95

Shepherd's PieServing: 8 97

Stuffed PeppersServing: 6 99

Beef and Potato StewServing: 10 100

Sloppy JoesServings: 8 102

Chili MacaroniServing: 8 104

Short Ribs in BBQ SauceServings: 8 105

Salisbury SteakServings: 6 106

Bacon Pork LoinServing: 8 108

LasagnaServing: 5 109

Dr. Pepper Pulled Pork Serving: 6-8 110

Lo MeinServings: 6 112

Pot RoastServing: 6 113

Beef RaguServing 8 115

Steak FajitasServings: 6 117

Chicken 118

Chicken and OrzoServing 4 118

Hawaiian ChickenServing 4 120

Chicken and MushroomsServing 4 121

Spicy Chicken and RiceServing 8 122

Chicken Rice CasseroleServing 6 123

Chicken TacosServing 8 124

Sweet Chili DrumsticksServing 6 125

JambalayaServing 6 127

Cashew ChickenServing 4 128

Chicken in Creamy SauceServing 4 129

Chicken AlfredoServing 6 131

Whole ChickenServing 2 132

Lettuce WrapsServing 6 133

Chicken StewServing: 4 134

Easy Chicken DinnerServing 4 135

Chicken StroganoffServing 4 137

Chicken Noodle CasseroleServing 6 138

Lemon Garlic ChickenServing 6 139

Sesame ChickenServing 4 141

Chicken SandwichesServing 6 142

Loaded PotatoesServing 6 144

Caramelized OnionsServing size 3 cups 146

Whole CauliflowerServing 6-8 147

Butternut squash Serving 8 148

Spinach LasagnaServing 6-8 149

Green Beans with HamServing 6 150

Sweet PotatoesServing 8 151

Pizza BakeServing 4 152

Ranch MushroomsServing 4 153

Creamed SpinachServing 5 154

Brown Rice and MushroomsServing 4 155

Baked BeansServing 6 156

Warm Brussels Sprouts SaladServing 8 157

Corn on the CobServing 2 159

Mashed PotatoesServing 8 160

Butter CarrotsServing 4 161

Garlic and Herb MushroomsServing 4 162

Scalloped PotatoesServing 8 163

Creamed CornServing 6 164

White Rice Serving 4 165

Mashed CauliflowerServing 6 166

Soups 167

Hearty VegetableServing 4 167

Toscana Soup Serving 6 168

Minestrone Serving 6-8 169

Lasagna Soup Serving 6-8 171

Creamy Tortellini Soup Serving 8 172

Bacon Corn Chowder Serving 8 173

Chicken Rice Soup Serving 8 175

Chicken Fajita Soup Serving 4 176

French Onion Soup Serving 8 177

Tomato Basil Soup Serving 8 179

Chili Serving 6 180

Chicken Noodle Serving 8 181

Ham and White Bean Soup Serving 10 182

White Chili Serving 6 184

Chicken Taco Soup Serving 6 185

Chicken Potato Soup Serving 6 187

Beef and Barley Soup Serving 4 188

Vegetable Beef Soup Serving 4 189

Stuffed Pepper Soup Serving 8 **Error! Bookmark not defined.**

Creamy Potato Soup Serving 6 **Error! Bookmark not defined.**

Plum Applesauce Serving 6 ...... **Error! Bookmark not defined.**

Part 1

Introduction

This book contains the best of crock-pot recipes for around the year and different meals of the day. As the name suggests, the book has 52 amazing recipes that are cooked in a crock-pot, so maybe you can try one special dish per week courtesy the recipes mentioned here.

Why crock-pot you ask? Well, simply because not all of us have the time to stand in front of the stove everyday and cook an elaborate meal. For people like us, the crockpot is a big boon, which cooks our meals in our absence. Just dump all the ingredients in the crock-pot and set the temperature as desired and watch culinary magic transpire right in front of your eyes.

This book contains 52 recipes that are divided as per your choice of meats like chicken, beef, turkey, lamb, pork as well as seafood. For the vegetarians, there is a wide range of recipes to choose from that will appeal to your dietary choices and taste buds. There are also a lot of soups included in this book, as they don't just make a healthy meal option but are extremely easy to cook.

So what are we waiting for, lets start rustling up the pot and get cooking.

PS: you can always add/take away specific ingredients if you think that will suit your palette and make your meals tastier/healthier.

Chapter 1: Crock-pot Soup Recipes

Lentil Soup:

Ingredients:

- 2 brown onions, finely chopped
- 4 sticks celery, trimmed, chopped coarsely
- 2 carrots, peeled, coarsely chopped
- 2 cloves garlic, crushed
- 2 swede, peeled, chopped coarsely
- 1 cup red lentils
- 4 cans tomatoes, diced
- 4 cups vegetable stock
- 6 teaspoons cumin, powdered
- 2 baguette (French loaf), sliced thinly diagonally
- 200 grams goat cheese

½ cup freshly chopped chives

Method:

1. Follow the manufacturer's instructions carefully and switch on the crock-pot.
2. Add onion, swede, garlic, carrots, lentil, tomato, and stock and cumin powder to the crock-pot.
3. Stir, cover and cook on Low for 6-7 hours or on High for 3 hours or the vegetables are tender and the lentil is cooked well.
4. In a small bowl, add goat cheese and chives. Mix well.

5. Meanwhile, preheat a grill. Place baguette slices on the baking tray. Grill the loaf for 2 minutes or until the sides are golden.
6. Spread the cheese-chive mixture on the loaf slices. Serve in individual soup bowls immediately with piping hot soup.

Turkey, Kale and Cauliflower Soup

Ingredients:

- 1 1/2 pounds ground turkey
- 2 1/2 cups cauliflower, grated or minced
- 6 cups kale, hard stems and ribs discarded, chopped
- 4 medium carrots, peeled, sliced
- 6 shallots, finely chopped
- 1 green bell pepper, finely chopped
- 1 red bell pepper, finely chopped
- 2 large tomatoes, chopped
- 8 cups chicken stock
- Salt to taste
- Pepper powder to taste

1 tablespoon coconut oil for greasing the pot

Method:

1. Follow the manufacturer's instructions carefully and switch on the crock-pot.
2. Add all the ingredients except kale to the crock-pot.
3. Stir, cover and cook on Low 6 hours or on High for 3 hours.
4. Add kale and mix well.
5. Cook for 15 to 20 minutes until the kale wilts.
6. Serve hot in individual soup bowls.

Potato and Corn Chowder

Ingredients:

- 12 ounces red potatoes, diced
- 8 ounces frozen corn
- 1 1/2 tablespoon all-purpose flour
- 4 cups chicken stock or any stock of your choice
- 1/2 teaspoon onion powder
- 1/4 teaspoon garlic powder
- 1/2 teaspoon dried oregano
- 1/2 teaspoon dried thyme
- Salt to taste
- Pepper powder to taste
- 2 tablespoons heavy cream

1 tablespoon unsalted butter

Method:

1. Follow the manufacturer's instructions carefully and switch on the crock-pot.
2. Whisk together about 1/2 a cup of stock and flour in a bowl and pour it into the crock-pot.
3. Add rest of the ingredients except cream and butter.
4. Stir, cover and cook on Low for 4 to 6 hours.
5. Add cream and butter. Mix well and serve immediately in individual soup bowls.

Baked Potato Soup

Ingredients:

- 2 pounds russet potatoes, peeled, chopped into small pieces
- 3 whole cloves garlic
- 4 cups chicken broth
- 1 medium onion, chopped
- 8 ounces low fat cream cheese
- 2 green onions, thinly sliced
- Salt to taste
    Pepper powder to taste

Method:

1. Follow the manufacturer's instructions carefully and switch on the crock-pot.
2. Add all the ingredients except cream cheese and green onions to the crock-pot.
3. Stir, cover and cook on Low for 7-8 hours or on High for 3-4 hours.
4. Retain about 1/4 of the soup and blend the rest of it with cream cheese.
5. Add green onions, reheat, mix well and serve.

Cheeseburger Soup

Ingredients:

- 1 1/2 pounds ground beef
- 1 1/2 cups onions, chopped
- 8 strips bacon, cooked, crumbled
- 1 1/2 cans (14 ounces each) diced tomatoes
- 3/4 cup celery, chopped
- 3 medium carrots, shredded
- 6 cloves garlic, minced
- 3 medium potatoes, peeled, cubed
- 6 cups chicken broth
- 1 1/2 cups milk
- 1/3 cup all-purpose flour
- 1 1/2 teaspoons dried parsley
- 1 1/2 teaspoons dried basil
- 1 1/2 teaspoons salt or to taste
   1/2 teaspoon pepper powder or to taste

Method:

1. Follow the manufacturer's instructions carefully and switch on the crock-pot.
2. Place a skillet over medium heat. Add onions and beef and sauté for a few minutes until the beef is not pink any more.
3. Transfer into a crock-pot.
4. Whisk together milk and flour in a small bowl and pour into the cooker.
5. Add rest of the ingredients except cheese.

6. Stir, cover and cook on Low for about 7 hours or on High for 3 1/2 to 4 hours
7. Add cheese and stir well.
8. Serve in individual soup bowls.

Irish Beef Soup

Ingredients:

- 1 pound beef stew meat, cubed
- 3 cups beef broth
- 1 cup water
- 1/3 cup pearl barley, rinsed, drained
- 1/2 an 8 ounces can tomato sauce
- 1/2 a 14 ounces can diced tomatoes
- 2 stalks celery, sliced into 1/2 inch pieces
- 1 medium onion, sliced
- 1 large carrot, peeled, sliced
- 1 bay leaf
- 1/2 teaspoon dried sage
- 1/4 teaspoon dried thyme
- 1/4 teaspoon pepper powder
    - 1/2 teaspoon salt or to taste

Method:

1. Follow the manufacturer's instructions carefully and switch on the crock-pot.
2. Add all the ingredients to the crock-pot.
3. Stir, cover and cook on Low for 7-8 hours or on High for 3-4 hours.
4. Serve hot in individual soup bowls.

Savory Cheese Soup

Ingredients:

- 7 ½ ounces broth (chicken or vegetable)
- 1 tablespoon red bell pepper, chopped
- 1 tablespoon onions, chopped
- 2 tablespoons celery, chopped
- 2 tablespoons carrots, chopped
- 1 teaspoon butter
- A pinch black pepper powder
- 1 tablespoon all-purpose flour
- 1 tablespoon cold water
- 1 ½ ounces cream cheese, cubed
- 6 tablespoons cheddar cheese, shredded
- 3 tablespoons beer or extra broth
  Croutons to serve

Method:

1. Follow the manufacturer's instructions carefully and switch on the crock-pot.
2. Add all the ingredients except croutons to the crock-pot.
3. Stir, cover and cook on Low for 3-4 hours.
4. Serve hot soup in individual soup bowls with croutons.

BBQ Chicken Soup

Ingredients:

- 1 pound chicken breast, skinless, boneless
- 1 medium onion, diced
- 2 cloves garlic, minced
- 1/2 a 15.5 ounce can white beans, drained, rinsed
- 1/2 a 15.5 ounce can corn with peppers
- 8 cups chicken broth
- 1/2 cup barbecue sauce
- 1/2 teaspoon salt or to taste
- 1/4 teaspoon pepper powder or to taste
  Cheddar cheese to serve (optional)

Method:

1. Follow the manufacturer's instructions carefully and switch on the crock-pot.
2. Pour broth, sauce, salt and pepper to the crock-pot. Mix well.
3. Add rest of the ingredients.
4. Stir, cover and cook on Low for 6 hours or on High for 3 hours.
5. Remove the chicken pieces from the cooker and set aside on a plate. When cool enough to handle, shred the chicken using a pair of forks.
6. Add the shredded chicken back to the crock-pot.
7. Cover and cook for another 30 minutes.
8. Serve in individual soup bowls garnished with cheddar cheese.

Mexican Chicken Soup:

Ingredients:

- ½ a whole chicken, skinless, chopped into pieces
- 4 cups chicken broth
- 2 carrots, peeled, sliced
- 1 small yellow onion, chopped
- 1 poblano pepper, chopped
- 2 cloves garlic, thinly sliced
- 2 roma tomatoes, chopped
- ½ cup tomato juice
- ½ teaspoon cumin
- ½ teaspoon ground coriander
- 1 tablespoon sea salt
- Juice of a lemon
- ¼ cup cilantro, chopped
- Cheddar cheese chips for serving

Method:

1. Follow the manufacturer's instructions carefully and switch on the crock-pot.
2. Add all the ingredients except cheddar cheese, lime juice, and cilantro into the crock-pot.
3. Stir, cover and cook on Low for 6 hours.
4. Remove the chicken pieces from the pot, remove the bone and shred the chicken with a fork.

5. Add the shredded chicken back to the pot. Add lime juice and cilantro.
6. Cook on Low for 2 more hours.
7. Meanwhile make the cheddar cheese chips as follows: Shred some cheddar cheese and place on a lined baking sheet. Bake at 400 degree F for 6-7 minutes. Remove from the oven and let it cool completely.
8. Serve hot soup in individual soup bowls with cheddar cheese chips.

Creamy Tomato Soup

Ingredients:

- 1 1/2 cups carrots, finely chopped
- 1 1/2 cups onions, finely chopped
- 1 1/2 cups celery, finely chopped
- 1/3 cup fresh basil
- 1 1/2 cans (28 ounces each) whole plum tomatoes with its juice, crushed
- 6 cups vegetable broth
- 3 teaspoons olive oil
- 1 1/2 teaspoons dried thyme
- 1 bay leaf
- 3 tablespoons unsalted butter
- 3 tablespoons flour
- 3 cups low fat milk, warmed
- 1/2 cup Pecorino Romano cheese
- Parmesan or Romano cheese rind (optional)
- Salt to taste
  Pepper powder to taste

Method:

1. Follow the manufacturer's instructions carefully and switch on the crock-pot.
2. Place a large skillet over medium heat. Add oil. When oil is heated, add onions, celery and carrots. Sauté until the onions are golden. Transfer into the crock-pot.

3. Add tomatoes, stock, thyme, basil, bay leaf and cheese rind.
4. Stir, cover and cook on Low for 6 hours or until done.
5. Discard cheese rind and bay leaf. Blend the soup.
6. Meanwhile, add butter to the skillet and add flour. Sauté for a couple of minutes and add about a cup of soup stirring constantly. Also add milk. Mix well and pour into the crock-pot.
7. Add cheese and stir well, reheat for about 5 minutes and serve immediately in individual soup bowls.

Chapter 2: Crock-pot Chicken Recipes

Roast Chicken & Potatoes:

Ingredients:

- 2 ½ pounds whole chicken, skinned
- 3 cloves garlic, sliced
- 1 onion, quartered
- 2-3 potatoes, scrubbed, prick all over with a fork
- 1 teaspoon kosher salt
- ½ teaspoon paprika
- ½ teaspoon onion powder
- ¼ teaspoon dried thyme
- ½ teaspoon Italian seasoning
- ¼ teaspoon cayenne pepper
- ¼ teaspoon pepper powder

1 tablespoon lemon juice for garnishing

Method:

1. Follow the manufacturer's instructions carefully and switch on the crock-pot.
2. Wrap the potatoes in foil. And place at the bottom of the slow cooker.
3. Pat dries the chicken with a paper towel.
4. Stuff the cavity of the chicken with onion and garlic.
5. Mix together rest of the ingredients together and rub the chicken with it.

6. Transfer the chicken into the cooker over the potatoes with the breast side down. Cover.
7. Cover and cook on Low for 8 hours or High for 4-5 hours.
8. To serve, remove the potatoes from the foil, sprinkle some lemon juice over the chicken and potatoes, and serve hot.

Crock-pot Chicken:

Ingredients:

- 1 small whole chicken, cleaned, pat dried
- 1 carrot, peeled, cut into pieces
- 1 stalk celery, chopped
- 1 medium onion, chopped
- 4 cloves garlic, peeled
- 1 tablespoon herbes de Provence
- Salt to taste
- Black pepper powder to taste
    Juice of a lemon

Method:

1. Follow the manufacturer's instructions carefully and switch on the crock-pot.
2. Stuff the chicken with garlic.
3. Sprinkle the chicken all over with salt, pepper and herbes de Provence.
4. Place the vegetables at the bottom of the crock-pot.
5. Place the chicken over the vegetables.
6. Cover and cook on Low for 6-8 hours or on High for 3-4 hours.
7. Sprinkle lemon juice and serve hot.

Sesame – Ginger Chicken:

Ingredients:

- ½ tablespoon sesame oil
- 4 bone in chicken thighs, skinned
- 1 tablespoon vegetable oil
- 2 tablespoons low sodium soy sauce
- 1 tablespoon light brown sugar
- 1 tablespoon fresh orange juice
- 2 ½ teaspoons hoisin sauce
- 1 tablespoon ginger, minced
- 2 cloves garlic
- ½ tablespoon corn starch
- ½ tablespoon water
- 1 teaspoon sesame seeds toasted
- 1 tablespoon green onion, sliced
  Cooking spray

Method:

1. Follow the manufacturer's instructions carefully and switch on the crock-pot.
2. Place a nonstick skillet over medium heat. Add oil and heat. Add chicken and cook on both sides until golden brown.
3. Spray the slow cooker with oil. Place the browned chicken in the cooker.
4. Mix together soy sauce, brown sugar, orange juice, hoisin sauce, ginger, and garlic. Pour this over the chicken.

5. Cover and cook on Low for 2 ½ to 3 hours. When cooked, transfer the chicken on to a platter and keep warm.
6. Strain the remaining liquid in the cooker and place in a pan (it should measure at least ½ to ¾ cup otherwise add water). Discard the solids.
7. Heat the saucepan over medium heat and bring to a boil. Mix together cornstarch and water in a small bowl. Add this to the saucepan. Stir constantly until thickened. Bring back to a boil.
8. Pour sauce over the chicken.
9. Sprinkle sesame seeds and green onions and serve immediately.

Creamy Chicken and Mushroom Potpie

Ingredients:

- 16 ounces cremini mushrooms, stems trimmed, halved if the mushrooms are large
- 8 carrots, peeled, cut into 1 inch pieces
- 3 pounds chicken thighs, skinless, boneless
- 1 large onion, chopped
- 2/3 cup all-purpose flour
- 2 sheets puff pastry, thawed
- 2 cups frozen green beans
- 2 cups frozen green peas
- 2 bay leaves
- 1 teaspoon dried thyme
- 1 cup water
- Salt to taste
- Pepper powder to taste
    - ¼ cup cream

Method:

1. Follow the manufacturer's instructions carefully and switch on the crock-pot.
2. Add onions, mushrooms, carrots, onion, all-purpose flour, thyme, bay leaves and water to the crock-pot. Stir the contents well.

3. Lay the chicken thighs over the vegetable mixture. Sprinkle salt and pepper over the chicken as well as over the vegetables.
4. Cover and cook on Low for 7 – 8 hours or on High for 4 – 5 hours.
5. When done, switch off the crock-pot and keep it covered.
6. Cut the pastry sheets with a 4-½ inch cutter into 4 circles. Place the circles on a baking sheet and bake in a preheated oven at 425 degree F for about 8 – 10 minutes.
7. Just before serving, add peas, green beans, cream and salt to the crock-pot.
8. Cover and heat the contents thoroughly.
9. Divide and serve chicken along with vegetables in individual serving bowls. Place a baked pastry round over each bowl and serve.

Hawaiian Chicken

Ingredients:

- 3 chicken breasts (about 1 1/4 pounds)
- 1/2 a 16 ounces can sliced pineapple, drained
- 1/2 a 15 ounces can mandarin oranges, drained
- 1/2 teaspoon ground ginger
- 2 tablespoon lemon juice
- 2 tablespoons corn starch
- 4 tablespoons brown sugar
- 4 tablespoons soy sauce
- Salt to taste
- Pepper powder to taste
    Cooking spray

Method:

1. Follow the manufacturer's instructions carefully and switch on the crock-pot.
2. Spray the crock-pot with cooking spray. Place the chicken breasts in the crock-pot.
3. Whisk together in a bowl, cornstarch, brown sugar, soy sauce, lemon juice, ginger, salt and pepper. Pour this mixture over the chicken.
4. Add the orange and pineapple slices.
5. Cover and cook on Low for 4-5 hours or on High for 2 - 3 hours.
6. Serve hot.

Chicken Paprikash

Ingredients:

- 1 pound chicken breast, skinless, boneless, cut into 1/2 inch strips
- 1 cup onion, chopped
- 2 teaspoons garlic, minced (preferably minced)
- 1 medium carrot, shredded
- 4 ounce mushrooms, sliced
- 1 medium red bell pepper, chopped
- 1 tablespoon Hungarian sweet paprika
- 1 1/2 tablespoons all-purpose flour
- 3/4 cup low sodium chicken broth
- Salt to taste
- Pepper powder to taste
    - 3/4 cup sour cream

Method:

1. Follow the manufacturer's instructions carefully and switch on the crock-pot.
2. Place chicken in a bowl and sprinkle flour all over it and coat it well. Transfer into the crock-pot.
3. Add rest of the ingredients except sour cream.
4. Stir, cover and cook on Low for 8 hours.
5. Add sour cream, stir and serve.

Chapter 3: Crock-pot Turkey Recipes

Turkey Osso Buco

Ingredients:

- 1 whole turkey legs, cut at joints into drumsticks and thighs, skinless
- 1/2 teaspoon dried thyme
- 1 medium onion, chopped
- 1 medium carrot, peeled, chopped
- 4 cloves garlic, minced, divided
- 1 stalk celery, chopped
- 1/2 tablespoon olive oil
- 1/4 cup dry red wine
- 14 ounce canned, diced tomatoes along with juice
- 2 tablespoons fresh Italian parsley, chopped
- 1/2 teaspoon lemon zest, grated
- Salt to taste
    Pepper powder to taste

Method:

1. Follow the manufacturer's instructions carefully and switch on the crock-pot.
2. Crush dried thyme and rub it all over the turkey. Season with salt and pepper. Place the turkey in a slow cooker.
3. Place a nonstick skillet over medium high heat. Add oil. When oil is hot, add onions, carrots, celery and

sauté for a few minutes until onions are translucent. Add half the garlic, sauté for a few minutes until fragrant. Transfer into the slow cooker.
4. To the same skillet, add wine and boil for a few seconds. Scrape any browned bits that may be stuck to the bottom of the skillet. Pour it to the cooker pot. Add tomatoes along with the juices.
5. Stir, cover and cook on Low for 10-11 hours or on High for 5 1/2 hours until the meat comes off the bone.
6. Mix together in a small bowl, parsley, lemon zest, and remaining garlic. Add salt and pepper, mix well and keep aside.
7. Remove the turkey from the pot with a slotted spoon. Pull apart the meat from the bones and serve in individual bowls. Top with vegetables and its liquid from the pot. Sprinkle the parsley mixture over it and serve.

Turkey Madeira

Ingredients:

- 3 pounds turkey breast tenders
- 4 ounces dried mushrooms
- 6 tablespoons Madeira wine
- 2 tablespoons lemon juice
- 1 1/2 cups chicken broth
- Salt to taste
- Pepper powder to taste
    2 tablespoons cornstarch mixed with 2-3 tablespoons water

Method:

1. Follow the manufacturer's instructions carefully and switch on the crock-pot.
2. Add all the ingredients except cornstarch mixture to the crock-pot.
3. Stir, cover and cook on Low for 7-8hours.
4. When done, pour the liquid remaining in the crock-pot to a skillet. Place the skillet over medium heat.
5. Add cornstarch mixture. Stir constantly until thickened. Pour over turkey and serve.

Turkey Pad Thai

Ingredients:

- 1 cup turkey, cubed
- 2 scallions, chopped
- 1 small onion, sliced
- 1/2 cup Napa cabbage, chopped, packed
- 1/2 cup Bok Choy, chopped, packed
- 1 cup broccoli slaw, packed
- 1/4 cup hot water
- 2 tablespoons sugar
- 1 tablespoon low sodium soy sauce
- 1 tablespoon rice vinegar
- 1/2 tablespoon chili garlic sauce
- 2 tablespoons lime juice
- 1/4 cup cilantro
- 2 cloves garlic, minced
  - 4 ounce whole wheat linguine, cooked according to instructions on the package

Method:

1. Follow the manufacturer's instructions carefully and switch on the crock-pot.
2. Add water, sugar, vinegar, and chili garlic sauce and lime juice. Mix well.
3. Add turkey and cover the turkey with the sauce mixture. Add rest of the ingredients.

4. Stir, cover and cook on Low for 6 hours or on High for 3 hours.
5. When done, add to the linguini. Toss well and serve.

Hearty Jambalaya

Ingredients:

- 1 can (14 ounce) tomatoes, diced, with its juices
- ½ pound fully cooked turkey sausage, cubed
- ¼ pound chicken breasts, boneless, skinned, cut into 1 inch cubes
- 4 ounce canned tomato sauce
- ½ cup onions, diced
- ½ a small red bell pepper diced
- ½ a small green bell pepper, diced
- ½ cup chicken broth
- 1 celery stalk, leaves, chopped
- 1 tablespoon tomato paste
- 1 teaspoon dried oregano
- 1 teaspoon Cajun seasoning
- 1 teaspoon garlic, minced
- 1 bay leaf
- ½ pound medium shrimps, cooked
- 1 teaspoon hot sauce
    Hot cooked rice to serve

Method:

1. Follow the manufacturer's instructions carefully and switch on the crock-pot.
2. Add all the ingredients except the shrimps and rice. Cover.

3. Set the cooker on low for 6-7 hours or until the chicken is cooked through.
4. Add shrimp. Cover and cook again for 15 minutes.
5. Discard bay leaves. Stir well.
6. Serve over hot rice.

Turkey Stew with Roasted Hatch chilies

Ingredients:

- 2 pounds free-range ground turkey or ground beef if you prefer beef
- 1 tablespoon extra-virgin olive oil
- 2 cloves garlic, chopped
- 1 medium red onion, chopped
- 1 cup roasted Hatch chilies, chopped
- 1 medium, peeled, cubed
- 1 ear of fresh sweet corn, cut off the cob
- ½ a 14-oz can fire roasted diced tomatoes
- 2 cups broth, or more if needed
- ½ teaspoon cumin
- ½ teaspoon ground coriander
- Sea salt to taste
- Ground pepper, to taste
- Juice of a lime
- Avocado, sliced to serve
- Sour cream to serve (optional)
    - Fresh cilantro to serve

Method:

1. To roast the chilies: Take some Mexican Hatch chilies and roast in the oven at 450 degrees for about 7 minutes. Alternately you can grill the chilies or sauté in a pan on high heat for about 10 minutes.

2. Follow the manufacturer's instructions carefully and switch on the crock-pot.
3. Place a skillet over medium heat. Add the ground turkey and cook until browned. Transfer the turkey into the crock-pot.
4. Add rest of the ingredients except lime, avocado, sour cream, and cilantro.
5. Stir, cover and cook on Low for 7-8 hours or on High for 3-4 hours.
6. When done add lime juice and sprinkle cilantro.
7. Serve with sour cream and avocado.

Mediterranean Roast Turkey

Ingredients:

- 1 cup onions, chopped
- 1/4 cup julienne cut, oil packed sun dried tomato halves drained
- 1/4 cup Kalamata olives, pitted
- 1 teaspoon garlic, minced
- 1 tablespoon fresh lemon juice
- 1/2 teaspoon Greek seasoning mix
- 1/4 teaspoon salt
- Freshly ground black pepper powder to taste
- 2 pound turkey breast, boneless, trimmed
- 1/4 cup fat free, low sodium chicken broth, divided
- 1 1/2 tablespoons all-purpose flour
  A few sprigs of thyme

Ingredients:

1. Follow the manufacturer's instructions carefully and switch on the crock-pot.
2. Add all the ingredients except flour and half the chicken broth to the slow cooker.
3. Stir, cover and cook on low for 7 hours.
4. Meanwhile, mix together flour and remaining broth until smooth. Pour into the cooker. Stir well, cover and cook on Low for 30 minutes more.
5. When done, chop the turkey into slices and serve.

Chapter 4: Crock-pot Beef Recipes

Korean Beef

Ingredients:

- 1 1/2 pounds beef chuck roast, cut into 1 inch cubes
- 1/2 cup beef broth
- 1/4 cup low sodium sauce
- 1/4 cup brown sugar, packed
- 1/2 tablespoon sesame oil
- 2 cloves garlic, minced
- 1/2 tablespoon fresh ginger, grated
- 1/2 tablespoon rice wine vinegar
- 1 teaspoon Sriracha sauce or to taste
- 1/2 teaspoon onion powder
- 1/4 teaspoon white pepper powder
- 1 tablespoon cornstarch
- 2 tablespoons water
- 1/2 teaspoon sesame seeds
  1 green onion, thinly sliced

Method:

1. Follow the manufacturer's instructions carefully and switch on the crock-pot.
2. Place the chuck roast in the crock-pot. Mix together in a bowl, beef broth, soy sauce, brown sugar, garlic, sesame oil, vinegar, ginger, onion powder, Sriracha

sauce and white powder. Pour this mixture into the crock-pot.
3. Stir, cover and cook on Low for 7-8 hours
4. Meanwhile, whisk together cornstarch and water. Add to the crock-pot. Mix well, cover and cook for another 30 minutes or until the sauce thickens.
5. Serve garnished with sesame seeds and green onions.

Slow cooked Spaghetti Sauce

Ingredients:

- 2 pounds ground beef
- 1/2 pound bulk Italian sausage
- 1 large onion, chopped
- 4 tablespoons olive oil
- 6 teaspoons garlic powder
- 1 teaspoon dried marjoram
- 2 teaspoons dried Italian seasoning
- 2 cans (29 ounces each) tomato sauce
- 2 cans (6 ounces each) tomato paste
- 2 cans (14.5 ounce each) Italian style diced tomatoes
- 2 cans (14.5 ounce each) Italian style stewed tomatoes
- 2 tablespoons sugar
- 1 teaspoon dried oregano
- 1/2 teaspoon dried thyme
    - 1/2 teaspoon dried basil

Method:

1. Follow the manufacturer's instructions carefully and switch on the crock-pot.
2. Place a nonstick skillet over medium heat. Add oil and heat. Add onions and sausage and cook until brown. Transfer into the crock-pot.

3. To the same skillet, add ground beef, Italian seasoning, marjoram and 2 teaspoons garlic powder. Cook until brown simultaneously breaking beef.
4. Transfer into the crock-pot. Add rest of the ingredients except sugar.
5. Stir, cover and cook on Low for 8 hours. Add sugar during the last 15 minutes of cooking.
6. Stir well and serve.

Salisbury steak

Ingredients:
- 1 pound lean ground beef
- ½ envelope (½ ounce) dry onion soup mix
- ¼ cup Italian seasoned bread crumbs
- 2 tablespoons milk
- 2 tablespoons all-purpose flour
- 1 tablespoons vegetable oil
- 1 (10.75 ounce) can condensed cream of chicken soup
- ½ packet (½ ounce) dry au jus mix
  6 tablespoons water

Method:

1. Follow the manufacturer's instructions carefully and switch on the crock-pot.
2. Mix together in a bowl, the ground beef, onion soup mix, breadcrumbs and milk. Mix well with your hands. Make patties.
3. Place a skillet over medium high heat. Add oil. Heat.
4. Coat the patties with flour. Place it in the skillet. Brown the patties.
5. Stack the patties in the slow cooker.
6. Meanwhile mix together in a bowl, the cream of chicken soup, au jus mix and water.
7. Pour this mixture over the stacked patties.
8. Set on Low and cook for 4-5 hours until the beef is cooked.

9. Serve with mashed potatoes.

Beef Nachos

Ingredients:

- 1 ½ pounds beef rump roast
- ½ a 12 ounce jar mild banana pepper rings
- ½ a 15 ounce can beef broth
- ½ tablespoon olive oil
- 2 cloves garlic, minced
- ½ a 15 ounce can black beans, rinsed
- 1 large ripe tomato, chopped
- 1 large onion, finely chopped
- Monterey Jack cheese, shredded to serve
- Tortilla chips to serve
- Sour cream to serve
- 2 tablespoons fresh cilantro, chopped
- 1 avocado, peeled, pitted, thinly sliced
- Salt to taste
    Pepper powder to taste

Method:

1. Follow the manufacturer's instructions carefully and switch on the crock-pot.
2. Sprinkle roast with salt and pepper.
3. Place a nonstick skillet over medium high heat. Add roast and cook until brown. Transfer into the crock-pot.
4. Add banana pepper rings, broth and garlic.

5. Stir, cover and cook on Low for 8 hours. Remove roast and place on your cutting board. When cool enough to handle, shred the meat and transfer it back to the pot. Stir and cook for another 5-7 minutes.
6. Meanwhile, lay tortilla chips on a baking sheet. Layer the chips with shredded beef, black beans, followed by tomatoes and onions and finally cheese.
7. Bake in a preheated oven at 350 degree F for about 10 minutes.
8. Garnish with cilantro and sour cream. Serve with avocado.

Italian Beef:

Ingredients:
- 1 ½ pounds beef chuck roast
- 1 ½ dry Italian salad dressing mix
- ½ cup water
- 8 ounce jar pepperoncini peppers
  4 hamburger buns, split
  Method:
1. Follow the manufacturer's instructions carefully and switch on the crock-pot.
2. Place the beef chuck roast in the crock-pot.
3. Add the Italian dressing mix.
4. Pour water. Cook on High for 6-7 hours.
5. In the last hour, shred the meat. If you are not able to shred it properly, cook for a longer time.
6. Add the peppers and some of the juice (optional).
7. Serve over the split buns.

Autumn Pot Roast

Ingredients:

- 1 1/2 pounds pot roast, lean, boneless, trimmed of fat
- 1 medium onion, sliced
- 3/4 pound sweet potatoes, peeled, quartered
- 1/2 tablespoon vegetable oil
- 1 teaspoon beef bouillon granules
- 1/2 cup water
- 1/4 teaspoon celery seeds
- A pinch ground cinnamon
- Salt to taste
- Pepper powder to taste
    1 tablespoon cornstarch mixed with 2 tablespoons water

Method:

1. Follow the manufacturer's instructions carefully and switch on the crock-pot.
2. Place a nonstick skillet over medium high heat. Add oil. When oil is heated, add roast and cook until brown. Transfer into the crock-pot.
3. Place onions and sweet potatoes over the roast.
4. Mix together the beef bouillon granules, cinnamon, celery seed, salt and pepper and water. Pour it over the roast.

5. Cover the mix and cook on Low for 8-10 hours or on High for about 4-5 hours.
6. Remove the meat and vegetables with a slotted spoon and place in a serving dish.
7. Transfer the liquid that was remaining in the crock-pot into a skillet. Place the skillet over medium heat and bring to a boil.
8. Add cornstarch mixture and stir constantly until thickened.
9. Pour sauce over roast and vegetables and serve.

Chapter 5: Crock-pot Pork Recipes

Spaghetti squash and Meatballs

Ingredients:

- 2 pounds ground Italian sausage
- 2 medium spaghetti squash, halved, deseeded
- 2 cans (14 ounces each) tomato sauce
- 1 teaspoon dried oregano
- 1 teaspoon dried basil
- 1 teaspoon thyme
- 8 cloves garlic, whole
- 4 tablespoons hot pepper relish (optional)
- 4 tablespoons olive oil
- 2 tablespoons fresh parsley, chopped

Method:

1. Follow the manufacturer's instructions carefully and switch on the crock-pot.
2. Add olive oil, tomato sauce, garlic, hot pepper relish, oregano, basil, and thyme to the cooker. Mix well.
3. Place the spaghetti squash halves in the cooker with its cut side down.
4. Meanwhile, make small meatballs with the ground meat and place it all around the squash.
5. Cover and set the cooker on Low for 4-5 hours or on High for 3 hours.

6. When done, remove the squash from the pot. When cool enough to handle, pull out the flesh from the squash using a large fork.
7. Place the squash flesh on a serving platter. Top with the meatballs. Pour the sauce all over. Garnish with parsley and serve hot.

Mexican Posole

Ingredients:

- 1 pound pork loin roast, boneless, cut into bite sized cubes
- 1 medium onion, sliced
- 1 can (15.5 ounce) white hominy, drained
- 1 can (14.5 ounce) enchilada sauce
- 3 cups water
- ½ tablespoon canola oil
- ¼ cup green chilies, sliced
- 2 cloves garlic, minced
- ¼ teaspoon cayenne pepper or to taste
- 1 teaspoon dried oregano
- Salt to taste
   2 tablespoons fresh cilantro, chopped

Method:

1. Follow the manufacturer's instructions carefully and switch on the crock-pot.
2. Place a nonstick skillet over medium high heat. Add oil. When oil is heated, add pork loin roast and cook until brown. Transfer into the crock-pot.

3. Pour enchilada sauce over it. Spread hominy, onions, garlic, cayenne pepper and oregano over it.
4. Pour water, cover and cook on Low for 10-12 hours or on High for 5-6 hours.

Portuguese Chorizo and Peppers

Ingredients:

- 1 pound chorizo sausage, remove the casing, crumbled
- 1 green bell pepper, deseeded, chopped
- ½ a 6 ounce can tomato paste
- ½ cup water
- ½ cup red wine
- 1 onion, peeled, chopped
    1 tablespoon garlic, crushed

Method:

1. Follow the manufacturer's instructions carefully and switch on the crock-pot.
2. Add all the ingredients to the crock-pot.
3. Stir, cover and cook on low for 6-7 hours.
4. Uncover and cook on Low for 2 more hours
5. Serve over hot rice.

Honey Soy Pork Tenderloin

Ingredients:

- 1 1/2 pounds pork tenderloin
- 2 tablespoons soy sauce
- 1/4 cup honey
- 2 tablespoons olive oil
- 1 1/2 tablespoons Montreal steak seasoning
- A large pinch ground ginger
- 1/4 teaspoon garlic powder
- A large pinch red pepper flakes
    Cooking spray

Method:

1. Follow the manufacturer's instructions carefully and switch on the crock-pot.
2. Spray the crock-pot with cooking spray.
3. Place the pork tender loin in the crock-pot.
4. Mix together in a bowl rest of the ingredients and pour over the pork in the crock-pot.
5. Cover and cook on LOW for 6 hours or on HIGH for 4 hours.

Szechuan Pork

Ingredients:

- 3 pounds lean pork chops, boneless, trimmed of fat
- 2 cans (8 ounces each) sliced water chestnuts, drained
- 2 cans (8 ounces each) sliced bamboo shoots, drained
- 12 green onions, sliced
- 3 tablespoons garlic, minced
- 4 tablespoons ginger, minced
- ½ cup soy sauce
- ½ cup Szechuan hot bean paste or sauce
- ½ cup Worcestershire sauce
- 4 tablespoons sesame oil
- 4 tablespoons rice wine or dry sherry
- 3 tablespoons sesame oil
- 3 tablespoons sugar
- 2 teaspoons hot sauce (optional)

Method:

1. Follow the manufacturer's instructions carefully and switch on the crock-pot.
2. Place a nonstick skillet over medium high heat. Add pork chops and cook until brown. Transfer into the crock-pot.

3. Place bamboo shoots over the chops, followed by water chestnuts and green onions.
4. Mix together rest of the ingredients in a bowl and pour it over the vegetables in the crock-pot.
5. Cover and cook on Low for 6-7 hours or on High for 3-4 hours.
6. Serve hot with steamed rice

Chapter 6: Crock-pot Lamb Recipes

Braised Lamb Shanks

Ingredients:

- 6 lamb shanks, trimmed of fat
- 1 large onion, chopped
- 3 carrots, peeled, chopped
- 3 stalks celery, chopped
- 1 ½ cups ripe tomatoes, peeled, deseeded, chopped
- 5 cloves garlic, crushed
- 3 cups chicken stock
- 3 tablespoons tomato paste
- 2 teaspoons fresh thyme
- 2 bay leaves
- 3 tablespoons olive oil
- 1 ½ cups red wine
- Salt to taste
    Pepper powder to taste

Method:

1. Follow the manufacturer's instructions carefully and switch on the crock-pot.
2. Sprinkle salt and pepper over the lamb shanks.
3. Place a nonstick skillet over medium high heat. Add oil. When oil is heated, add lamb shanks and cook until brown. Transfer into the crock-pot.

4. Add wine to the skillet and place over medium heat. Scrape any brown bits from the bottom of the skillet. Simmer for a couple of minutes and transfer into the crock-pot.
5. Add rest of the ingredients.
6. Stir, cover and cook on High for 6-7 hours. When done, transfer on to a serving dish.
7. Discard the bay leaf. Blend the remaining ingredients of the crock-pot until smooth.
8. Pour over the shanks and serve.

Slow cooked leg of lamb:

Ingredients:

- 1 ¾ pound leg of lamb, preferably bone out
- 2 tablespoons olive oil
- ¼ cup lemon juice
- 4 cloves garlic, crushed
- ½ teaspoon dried oregano
- ½ teaspoon ground nutmeg
- 1 teaspoon dried mint leaves
    - 2 tablespoons white vinegar

Method:

1. Follow the manufacturer's instructions carefully and switch on the crock-pot.
2. Mix together all the ingredients except the lamb, mint, and vinegar in the crock-pot.
3. Coat the leg of lamb with this mixture.
4. Cover and cook on High for 6-8 hours or until the meat is coming off the bone.
5. With a fork, shred the meat.
6. Sprinkle vinegar over the meat. Garnish with mint and serve hot.

Moroccan Lamb

Ingredients:

- 1 whole lamb shank, trimmed
- 1 medium onion, chopped
- 1 small red bell pepper, chopped
- 1/2 a 14 ounces can diced tomatoes
- 1/4 cup whole olives, drained
- 1/2 cup canned garbanzo beans, rinsed, drained
- 1/2 lemon, chopped into pieces
- 2 cloves garlic, minced
- 1/2 teaspoon sugar
- 1/2 teaspoon ground cumin
- 1/2 teaspoon ground coriander
- 1/2 teaspoon salt or to taste
- Pepper powder to taste
- 1 cup water
- 2 teaspoons olive oil
- 1 stick cinnamon (about an inch)
  2 tablespoons golden raisins

Method:

1. Follow the manufacturer's instructions carefully and switch on the crock-pot.
2. Mix together in a bowl, lemon, sugar and salt and set aside.
3. Season the lamb shank with salt and pepper.

4. Place a skillet over medium heat. Add olive oil. When oil is heated, add lamb shank and brown on all the sides. Remove from the pan and set aside.
5. To the same pan, add onions, bell pepper and garlic. Sauté for a couple of minutes and transfer into the crock-pot.
6. Add rest of the ingredients except raisins and mix well. Add lamb and coat it with the mixture in the pot.
7. Cover and cook on Low for 8-9 hours or on High for 4-5 hours.
8. Mid way through cooking, add raisins and the lemon mixture to it. Mix well and cover again.
9. When done, discard cinnamon and the lemon pieces and serve.

Irish Lamb Stew

Ingredients:

- 3 pounds leg of lamb, boneless, trimmed of fat, cut into 1 inch pieces
- 5 large leeks, white parts only, thinly sliced
- 2 1/2 pounds white potatoes, peeled, cut into 1 inch pieces
- 5 large carrots, peeled, cut into 1 inch pieces
- 4 stalks celery, thinly sliced
- 1 1/2 cans (14 ounces each) low sodium chicken broth
- 3 teaspoons fresh thyme, chopped
- 1/3 cup fresh parsley, chopped
- Salt to taste
    Pepper powder to taste

Method:

1. Follow the manufacturer's instructions carefully and switch on the crock-pot.
2. Add all the ingredients except parsley to the crock-pot.
3. Cover and cook on LOW for 7-8 hours or until done.
4. When done add parsley, mix well and serve.

Slow cooked Lamb Roast with Root Vegetables

Ingredients:

- 2 pounds lamb leg roast, boneless
- 1 parsnip, peeled, chopped
- 1 carrot, peeled, chopped
- 1 small rutabaga, peeled, chopped
- 1 Yukon gold potato, peeled, chopped
- ½ tablespoon ghee
- 3 cloves garlic, minced
- ¼ cup chicken broth
- 2 sprigs fresh rosemary, chopped
- 2 sprigs fresh thyme, chopped
- ¼ cup stone ground mustard
- Salt to taste
- Pepper powder to taste
   Green salad to serve

Method:

1. Follow the manufacturer's instructions carefully and switch on the crock-pot.
2. Sprinkle salt and pepper over the lamb shanks.
3. Place a cast iron skillet over medium high heat. Add ghee. When ghee is melted, add lamb roast and cook until brown. Transfer into the crock-pot.
4. Add broth to the skillet and place over medium heat. Scrape any brown bits from the bottom of the skillet. Simmer for a couple of minutes and set aside.
5. Mix together in a bowl, garlic, rosemary, thyme and mustard. Pour this mixture over the lamb. Mix well.

6. Add all the root vegetables to a large bowl. Season with salt and pepper. Toss well and place the root vegetables all around the lamb. Pour broth that was kept aside.
7. Cover and cook on Low for 8-10 hours.
8. Serve with green salad.

Smoky Spiced Lamb Chops

Ingredients:

- 2 large lamb chops
- ½ a yellow bell pepper, sliced
- ½ a red bell pepper, sliced
- 1 small onion, sliced into rings
- ½ teaspoon ground coriander
- 1 teaspoon smoked paprika or to taste
- ½ teaspoon ground cumin
- ¼ cup chicken broth
  Salt to taste

Method:

1. Follow the manufacturer's instructions carefully and switch on the crock-pot.
2. Place the onion rings at the bottom of the crock-pot. Place the lamb chops over it. Sprinkle, paprika, coriander, cumin and salt over it.
3. Place the bell pepper over it. Pour broth all around the chops.
4. Cover and cook on Low for 7-8 hours or on High for 4-6 hours.

Chapter 7: Crock-pot Seafood Recipes

Slow cooker Thai Green Fish Curry

Ingredients:

- 2 pounds firm white fish, chopped into cubes
- 1 large onion, chopped
- 2 green chilies, deseeded, finely chopped
- 4 tablespoons Thai green curry paste or add according to your taste
- 4 tablespoons sunflower oil
- 4 cm piece fresh ginger or galangal, peeled, finely chopped
- 2 tablespoons fish sauce
- Juice of 2 lemons
- 3 cups coconut milk
- 2 cups vegetable stock
- 6 spring onions, thinly sliced,
- 6 carrots, peeled, chopped into bite sized pieces
- 2 sprigs Thai basil leaves, finely chopped
- Salt to taste
- Pepper powder to taste
- A large pinch ground nutmeg
- 1 cup fresh cilantro leaves, chopped

Method:

1. Follow the manufacturer's instructions carefully and switch on the crock-pot.

2. Place a skillet over medium heat. Add oil. When oil is heated, add onions, chili and ginger. Sauté for 3*4 minutes until the onions are translucent.
3. Add curry paste, fish sauce, lime juice and nutmeg. Sauté for a couple of minutes. Add coconut milk and stock and bring to a boil. Add fish and carrots. Stir well and transfer into the crock-pot.
4. Add salt and pepper. Stir well.
5. Cover and cook on Low for 4 – 5 hours or on High for 3 hours.
6. Just before serving, add spring onions, cilantro and Thai basil leaves. Stir well and serve immediately.

Low country Boil

Ingredients:

- 3/4 pound small red potatoes, halved
- 1/2 pound kielbasa sausage, cooked, cut into bite sized pieces
- 1 pound raw, large shrimp in shells
- 2 fresh cobs of corn, cut into 3 inch pieces
- 1 stalk celery, chopped
- 2 small onions, quartered
- 2 cloves garlic minced
- 8 ounce broth
- 2 1/2 cups water
- 2 tablespoons Old bay seasoning
- 1 tablespoon Cajun seasoning
- 1 lemon, halved
  Cooking spray

Method:

1. Follow the manufacturer's instructions carefully and switch on the crock-pot.
2. Spray the crock-pot with cooking spray. Add water, broth, seasonings and garlic. Mix well.
3. Add potatoes, onions and celery. Squeeze the juice of lemon over it and place the rinds in the cooker.
4. Cover and cook on LOW for 4 hours.
5. Add corncobs and sausages. Cover and cook on LOW for 2 hours.

6. Add shrimp.
7. Cover and cook on HIGH for 40 minutes.
8. Drain the liquid that is in the crockpot using a colander.
9. Transfer on to a serving platter. Sprinkle some more Cajun seasoning and lemon juice and serve.

Shrimp Arrabbiata

Ingredients:

- 2 pounds frozen shrimp
- 2 onions, chopped
- 1 red bell pepper, chopped
- 1 green bell pepper, chopped
- 12 ounce spaghetti
- ½ teaspoon crushed red pepper
- 2 teaspoons dried oregano
- 2 teaspoons dried basil
- 2 cans tomato puree
- 6 cloves garlic, minced
   Salt to taste

Method:

1. Follow the manufacturer's instructions carefully and switch on the crock-pot.
2. Add onions, bell peppers, crushed pepper, oregano, basil, garlic, and tomato puree to the crock-pot.
3. Stir, cover and cook on Low for 2 hours. Add shrimp and cook on Low for 1 hour.
4. Add spaghetti. Mix well and serve.

Seafood Stew

Ingredients:

- 1 pound scallops
- 1 pound large shrimp
- 1 pound crab legs
- 1 1/2 pounds baby potatoes
- 1 large onion, chopped
- 1 1/2 cans (28 ounces each) crushed tomatoes
- 5 cloves garlic, minced
- 6 cups vegetable broth
- 3/4 cup white wine
- 1 1/2 teaspoons dried basil
- 1 1/2 teaspoons dried thyme
- 1 1/2 teaspoons dried cilantro
- 3/4 teaspoon celery salt
- 1/2 teaspoon red pepper flakes
    - 1/4 teaspoon cayenne pepper

Method:

1. Follow the manufacturer's instructions carefully and switch on the crock-pot.
2. Add all the ingredients except seafood to the crock-pot.
3. Cover and cook on LOW for 4-5 hours or until the potatoes are cooked.
4. When done add the seafood, mix well.

5. Cover and cook on HIGH for 30 minutes. Stir in between a couple of times.
6. Serve warm with toasted bread.

Lemony Shrimp Risotto

Ingredients:

- 3 cups Arborio rice or medium grain rice
- 3 teaspoons lemon zest, grated
- 1/3 cup lemon juice
- 1 ½ cups frozen green peas
- 1 ½ pounds medium shrimp, peeled, deveined
- 2 shallots, chopped
- 3 cans chicken broth
- 3 teaspoons butter
- ¾ cup dry white wine
- 3 teaspoons olive oil
- Salt to taste
    Pepper powder to taste

Method:

1. Follow the manufacturer's instructions carefully and switch on the crock-pot.
2. Place a nonstick skillet over medium heat. Add oil. When oil is heated, add shallots. Sauté until shallots turn translucent. Transfer into the crock-pot.
3. Add lemon juice, lemon zest, broth, wine and 2 cups of water to a saucepan and bring to a boil.
4. Transfer into the crock-pot. Add rice and stir well.
5. Cover and cook on Low for 5-6 hours or on High for 2 ½ to 3 hours.

6. Add frozen peas and shrimp. Cover and cook for about 30 minutes or until the shrimp turns opaque. Stir just once while cooking.
7. Stir the risotto well and serve.

Seafood Gumbo:

Ingredients:

- ¼ pound sliced bacon, diced
- 1 stalk celery, sliced
- 1 medium onion, sliced
- 1 cup green pepper, chopped
- 2 cloves garlic, minced
- 1 cup chicken broth
- ½ a 14 ounce can diced tomatoes
- 1 tablespoon Worcestershire sauce
- 1 teaspoon kosher salt or to taste
- 1 teaspoon dried thyme
- ½ pound large shrimps, cleaned
- ½ pound crabmeat
  5 ounce frozen okra, sliced lengthwise into ½ inch pieces

Method:

1. Follow the manufacturer's instructions carefully and switch on the crock-pot.
2. Place a skillet over medium heat. Add bacon and cook until the bacon is crisp. When done, transfer to the crock-pot. Discard the fat in the skillet.
3. To the same skillet, add celery, onions, pepper, and garlic. Sauté until the onions are translucent. Transfer to the crock-pot.

4. Add broth, tomatoes along with the liquid, Worcestershire sauce, salt, and thyme.
5. Set the crock-pot on Low for 4 hours or on High for 2 hours.
6. Add shrimps, crabmeat, and okra. Set the crock-pot on Low for 1 more hour or ½ an hour on High.
7. Stir well and serve.

Chapter 8: Crock-pot Vegetarian Recipes

Mixed Vegetable Curry:

Ingredients:

- 2 carrots, medium sized, sliced
- 1 potato, cut into ½ inch cubes
- ½ can (7.5 ounce) chick peas, drained, rinsed
- 4 ounces fresh beans, stringed, cut into 1 inch pieces
- ½ cup onion, coarsely chopped
- 2 cloves garlic, minced
- 1 tablespoon quick cooking tapioca
- 1 teaspoon curry powder
- ¼ teaspoon red chili flakes
- Salt to taste
- ½ teaspoon coriander, powdered
- 1 big pinch cinnamon powder
- 7 ounce vegetable broth
- ½ can (7 ¼ ounce) tomatoes (do not drain), chopped
    Hot cooked rice
    Method:
1. Follow the manufacturer's instructions carefully and switch on the crock-pot.

2. Add carrots, potatoes, onions, chickpeas, green beans, tapioca, garlic, and coriander, chili flakes, salt and cinnamon to the crock-pot.
3. Pour the vegetable broth over it.
4. Site, cover and cook on Low for 7-9 hours or on High for 3 ½ to 4 hours
5. Add the tomatoes along with the liquid. Stir well
6. Keep covered for 5 minutes.
7. Serve over hot rice.

Cauliflower Bolognese with Zucchini Noodles

Ingredients:

For the Bolognese:
- 2 heads cauliflower, chopped into florets
- 1 large onion, diced
- 4 cloves garlic, minced
- 2 cans (28 ounces each) diced tomatoes, unsalted
- ½ teaspoon red pepper flakes
- 4 teaspoons dried oregano
- 2 teaspoons dried basil flakes
- Salt to taste
- Pepper powder to taste

For the noodles:
> 6 large zucchini, made into noodles using a spiralizer or julienne peeler

Method:

1. Follow the manufacturer's instructions carefully and switch on the crock-pot.
2. Add cauliflower, onion, garlic, tomatoes, oregano, basil, red pepper flakes, salt and pepper to the crock-pot.
3. Cover and cook on Low for 4 - 5 hours or on High for 3 ½ hours.
4. When done, mash the cauliflower with a potato masher.

5. Place the zucchini noodles in large individual serving bowls. Place the Bolognese over it and serve.

Chinese Tofu and Vegetables

Ingredients:

For vegetables:
- 2 pounds extra firm tofu, chop into 1/2 inch thick slices
- 5-6 stalks of broccoli (florets not needed), slice into 1/4 inch round thick slices
- 2 cans (8 ounces each) sliced water chestnuts
- 4 medium zucchini, cut into 1/2 inch cubes
- 1 medium red bell pepper, cut into 1 inch squares
- 1 medium green bell pepper, cut into 1 inch squares
- Cooking spray

For the sauce:
- 1 large onion, minced
- 6 cloves garlic, minced
- 2 tablespoons fresh ginger, minced
- 1/2 cup hoisin sauce
- 2 cups tomato sauce, unsalted
- 1 teaspoon Worcestershire sauce
- 1/4 cup seasoned rice wine vinegar
- 2 tablespoons light soy sauce
- 4 teaspoons molasses
- 1/4 cup water
- 2 tablespoons spicy brown mustard
- 1/2 teaspoon crushed red pepper
- 1/2 teaspoon five spice powder

- Black pepper powder to taste
    Salt to taste

Method:
1. Follow the manufacturer's instructions carefully and switch on the crock-pot.
2. Place the tofu slices on paper towels and press lightly to remove excess liquid from tofu. Once it is done chop into triangles.
3. Spray the inside of the crock-pot with cooking spray.
4. Place a nonstick skillet over medium heat. Spray with cooking spray. Add tofu slices in batches and cook on both the sides until brown. Transfer into the crock-pot.
5. To make the sauce: To the same skillet, spray a little more oil. Add onions, garlic and ginger. Sauté until onions are translucent.
6. Add rest of the ingredients, mix well and bring to a boil. Transfer the sauce into the crock-pot and pour over the tofu pieces.
7. Cover and cook on Low for 5-6 hours or on High for 2 ½ - 3 hours. Add the vegetables into the pot. Mix well. Cover and cook on High for an hour. Serve over brown rice.

Enchilada Quinoa

Ingredients:

- ½ a 15 ounce can black beans, drained, rinsed
- 1 can (15 ounce) mild or medium red enchilada sauce, divided
- ½ a 15 ounce can yellow corn, drained, rinsed
- ½ a 15 ounce can diced fire roasted tomatoes with green chilies
- ½ cup quinoa, uncooked
- ¼ cup water
- 2 ounces Mexican cheese, shredded
- 2 tablespoons fresh cilantro, chopped
- 2 tablespoons sour cream
- 2 tomatoes, chopped
    1 avocado, peeled, pitted, sliced

Method:

1. Follow the manufacturer's instructions carefully and switch on the crock-pot.
2. Add all the beans, corn, and 1/2 can enchilada sauce; fire roasted tomatoes, quinoa, water and half the cheese to the crock-pot. Mix well.
3. Pour the remaining enchilada sauce on top. Sprinkle the remaining cheese.
4. Cover and cook on Low for 4 -5 hours or on High for 2-3 hours.
5. Serve hot.

Mediterranean Stew:

Ingredients:

- ½ butternut squash, peeled, deseeded, cubed
- 1 cup eggplants, cubed
- 1 cup zucchini, cubed
- ½ a 10 ounce package frozen okra, thawed
- ½ an 8 ounce can tomato sauce
- ½ cup onions, chopped
- 1 tomato, chopped
- 1 carrot, thinly sliced
- ½ cup low sodium vegetable broth
- 3 tablespoons raisins
- A large pinch cinnamon powder
- ¼ teaspoon turmeric powder
- Red chili flakes to taste
- ¼ teaspoon cumin powder
    A large pinch paprika

Method:

1. Follow the manufacturer's instructions carefully and switch on the crock-pot.
2. Add butternut squash, eggplant, zucchini, okra, tomato sauce, onions, tomato, carrot, vegetable broth, raisins, cinnamon powder, turmeric powder, red chili flakes, cumin powder and paprika to the crock-pot.
3. Stir, cover and cook on low for 8 hours or on high for 3-4 hours.

Vegetarian Chili:

Ingredients:

- ½ a 19 ounce can low sodium black bean soup
- ½ a 15 ounce can kidney beans, unsalted, rinsed, drained
- ½ a 15 ounce can garbanzo beans, unsalted, rinsed, drained
- ½ a 16 ounce can vegetarian baked beans, low beans
- ½ a 14.5 ounce can chopped tomatoes, pureed
- ½ a 15 ounce can whole corn kernels, drained
- 1 onion, chopped
- ½ a green bell pepper, chopped
- ½ a red bell pepper, chopped
- 1 stalk celery, chopped
- 2 cloves garlic, chopped
- ½ tablespoon chili powder to taste
- ½ tablespoon dried oregano
- ½ tablespoon dried parsley
- ½ tablespoon dried basil
- Salt to taste
    Pepper powder to taste

Method:

1. Follow the manufacturer's instructions carefully and switch on the crock-pot.

2. Add black bean soup, kidney beans, garbanzo beans, baked beans, tomatoes, corn kernels, onion, green bell pepper, red bell pepper, celery, garlic, chili powder, oregano, parsley and dried basil.
3. Cover and cook on Low for 5-6 hours or on High for 2-2 ½ hours.
4. Serve over rice or with toasted bread.

Conclusion

With this, we come to the end of this book. I shared 52 recipes, one for each week of the year. I sincerely hope you found these recipes easy to cook and enjoy great meals with your family.

All the recipes mentioned in the book are healthy and almost all ingredients are easily available. Thanks to these recipes, now you have the chance to showcase your culinary skills to your family and friends, that too without spending hours in the kitchen. All you need is your prep time and that's about it. Let the crockpot work its magic.

So let's not waste anymore time and get cooking. Thank you once again for choosing this book.

Part 2

Introduction

Don't be in such a rush to push your slow cooker into the darkest corner of your kitchen!

It is still one of the best appliances in there! Wipe off that dust and prepare to be amazed!

So many delicious recipes can be made in this magic pot. Especially if you are about to serve a crowd, I mean a family!

It is always so super easy: you load it, turn it on and forget about it...for a while (not if you are cooking in it for the first time though!!!). But, just think about it, with a push of one button, and a correct mix of the ingredients (!), you can have a meal, a side dish, soup or a dessert ready, without actually doing anything!

This time we prepared an amazing list of meals that can be made even by a newbie! Some of them are very simple and some of them are regular crowd-pleasers. All of the recipes are totally adjustable, make more-make less; the food will come out delicious!

Meat

BBQ Beef Brisket Serving: 6-8

Prep Time: 10 min Cook Time: 8 hrs

Ingredients

3 lbs beef brisket (no fat)
1 ½ cup BBQ sauce
3 tbsp Worcestershire sauce
1 ½ tsp liquid smoke flavoring
1 tsp onion powder
1 tbsp smoked paprika
1 tbsp dried thyme
½ tsp garlic powder
½ tsp cayenne pepper
½ tsp ground cumin
Salt, pepper

Directions

Coat the brisket with liquid smoke flavoring. Rub to cover all of it.
Mix the seasonings and cover the brisket with the mix.

Pour Worcestershire and BBQ sauce to the bottom of the slow cooker. Set the brisket on top.

Cook on low for 8-9 hours, until the meat is tender and pull apart easily.

Shred and serve with your favorite side!

Red Beans and Sausage Serving: 10

Prep Time: 12 min Cook Time: 8 hrs

Ingredients

- 1 lbs sausage
- 1 lbs dry red kidney beans
- 1 onion
- 1 bell pepper
- 3 celery stalks
- 3 garlic cloves
- 1 tsp hot sauce
- ½ tsp dried thyme
- 2 bay leaves
- 7 cup water
- 10 cup cooked rice
- Salt, pepper

Directions

Rinse the beans. Place in the slow cooker.

Dice onion and pepper. Cut up celery. Mince the garlic. Load in the slow cooker. Add in sausage. Season with thyme, salt, pepper. Throw in a couple bay leaves, pour in the water. Cook on high for 6 hours (10 on low).

In the last 2 hours start cooking rice (in the rice cooker or the stove top, it's up to you).

Serve the beans and sausage over rice!

Beef Tips in Gravy Servings: 6

Prep Time: 15 min   Cook Time: 6 hrs

Ingredients

3 lbs top sirloin
3 tbsp oil
2 cups beef broth
1 tbsp Worcestershire sauce
Italian seasoning, dried thyme, salt, pepper
1 cup diced onion
1 tbsp minced garlic
3 tbsp water
2 tbsp cornstarch
Bay leaf

Directions

Cut up the beef in small cubes.
On the stove top Heat 1 tbsp of oil and cook the beef until it's lightly brown. Season, with salt and pepper, to taste.
Transfer to the slow cooker. Pour in the beef broth and Worcestershire sauce. Drop in a bay leaf. Sprinkle with Italian seasoning and thyme. Add the diced onions and minced garlic to the top.
Cook on high for 3-4 hours (6-7 on low).
When the time is up, mix water and cornstarch and pour in the slow cooker and stir in. Set for additional 10 min to thicken the gravy. Scoop out the bay leaf.
Serve hot over mashed potatoes or rice!

Beef Enchiladas

Servings: 12

Prep Time: 20 min Cook Time: 8 hrs 30 min

Ingredients

- 2 lbs chuck roast
- 2 cup beef broth
- 2 tbsp apple cider vinegar
- 1 cup salsa
- Ground cumin, chili powder, onion and garlic powder
- 2 tbsp cornstarch
- 2 tbsp water
- 10 small tortillas
- 1 cup shredded cheddar
- 1 cup shredded Monterey jack
- Salt, pepper

Directions

Rub salt and pepper all over the roast so all the sides are evenly covered. Set it to the bottom of the slow cooker. Combine broth, vinegar, salsa and seasonings. Pour on top over the roast. Cook on low for 8 hours.

When the roast is done transfer it to the plate and shred.

Pour the remaining broth mix into the pan. Mix cornstarch and water and stir into the broth. Adjust the seasonings. Cook until the mixture thickens.

Preheat the oven to 350 degrees F.

Mix half the broth mixture with shredded beef. Fill each tortilla with a spoonful of beef and a spoonful of cheese. Roll and lay out in a baking dish. Repeat until tortillas and meat is gone. Pour the rest of the broth mix over the enchiladas and sprinkle the remaining cheese on top.

Bake for 30 min, until it starts bubbling.

Let cool for 10 min before serving!

Stuffed Meatballs

Servings: 4-6

Prep Time: 15 min Cook Time: 3 hrs

Ingredients

- 1lbs ground beef
- 1 cup bread crumbs
- 4 mozzarella sticks
- 1 egg
- 1 egg yolk
- 2 tsp garlic powder
- 1 tsp onion powder
- 1 tbsp Italian seasoning
- Salt, pepper
- 1 jar marinara sauce

Directions

Cut the cheese sticks in half and set in the freezer until you need them.

In a large bowl, mix beef with breadcrumbs, egg and egg yolk. Sprinkle with Italian seasoning, onion and garlic powder, salt and pepper. It is easier to mix with your hands, but you can try other ways.

Pull the cheese out of the freezer.

Get a handful of meat mix and place a piece of cheese in the middle. Cover the cheese with the meat and roll into a ball. Make sure no cheese is showing. Repeat until the meat is gone.

Cook on high for 1-2 hours (on low 3-4 hours).

Sprinkle with some extra Italian seasoning and serve with a side of marinara!

Taco Lasagna Servings: 6

Prep time: 15 min

Cook time: 4 hrs

Ingredients

2 lbs ground beef
1 cup salsa
1 can black beans
1 pkg cream cheese
1 can enchilada sauce
3 cup shredded cheddar
4 large tortillas
Mix of diced tomatoes and chopped cilantro
3 tbsp taco seasoning
Sour cream

Directions

Brown up beef in the pan. Drain the grease and stir in salsa and some taco seasoning.

Mix the cream cheese with remaining taco seasoning until smooth. Add in the black beans.

Pour 1/3 cup of enchilada sauce to the bottom of the slow cooker. Place a tortilla shell in. Divide the meat and cream cheese in 3 parts. Start layering with beef; then cream cheese and beans; then cheese and enchilada sauce. Make 3 layers.

Cook on high for 3 hours (low for 4-5hrs).

Cut like a cake in 6. Serve with sour cream on the top!

Shepherd's Pie Serving: 8

Prep Time: 20 min Cook Time: 5 hrs

Ingredients

1 ½ lbs boneless chuck roast
4 carrots
8 oz white mushrooms
1 cup corn (thawed)
1 cup peas (thawed)
¾ cup beef broth
6 tbsp tomato paste
2 tsp Worcestershire sauce
3 tbsp flour
6 tbsp water
Oregano, salt, pepper, garlic and onion powder

Mashed potatoes:
2 lbs potatoes
1 cup warm milk
6 tbsp butter
1 ½ cup cheddar cheese
Salt, pepper

Directions

Trim the fat of the beef and cut into cubes. Slice the carrot.

Lay out the meat to the bottom of the slow cooker, top with carrots, mushrooms and corn.

Mix together Worcestershire sauce and beef broth. Add the seasonings. Pour in the slow cooker and mix well.

Cook on high for 3-4 hours (low for 7-9).

Mix flour and water. Whisk until smooth. Add in the slow cooker. Stir well. Add in the peas.

Make the mashed potatoes.

Boil potatoes until soft. Drain the water. Add warm milk and butter. Mash the potatoes. Add salt and pepper, to taste.

Add cheddar cheese to the mashed potatoes. Spread potatoes on top of the beef and veggies.

Cook for extra 25 min on high, so that the gravy thickens up. Serve!

Stuffed Peppers
Serving: 6

Prep Time: 15 min Cook Time: 6 hrs

Ingredients

6 bell peppers
1 ½ lbs ground beef
Small onion
1 ½ cup cooked rice
1 ¼ cup cheddar
2 garlic cloves
2 tbsp olive oil
1 can tomato sauce
Salt, pepper

Directions

Cut the tops off the peppers and clean out the seeds. Dice the onion and mince garlic.

Heat oil in a pan on the stove top. Cook onion until soft, add in garlic and cook for another minute.

Mix rice with ground beef. Add in onion and garlic mix. Stuff peppers with meat mix.

Set the peppers in the slow cooker. Pour tomato sauce over each one. Cook on low for 6 hours. On the last 30 min sprinkle the peppers with cheese.

Serve as a separate meal of with a side!

Beef and Potato Stew Serving: 10

Prep Time: 15 min Cook Time: 8 hrs

Ingredients

- 2 lbs lean beef stew meat
- 3 potatoes
- ¼ cup flour
- 1 can diced tomatoes
- 1 onion
- 2 tbsp olive oil
- 1 ½ cup beef broth
- 2 tsp Worcestershire sauce
- 1 garlic clove
- Bay leaf
- Salt, pepper, dried oregano, paprika

Directions

Dice the meat in the small cubes.

Combine flour, salt, pepper. Coat the beef in the flour mix.

Heat olive oil in the pan and brown up the meat. No need to cook it through, just until it gets brown on the outside.

Dice the onion and mince garlic. Cut up potatoes in cubes.

Transfer the meat with the grease from the pan to the slow cooker. Add in onion, garlic, potatoes, Worcestershire sauce and tomatoes along with the juice.

Mix broth with vinegar, sprinkle with oregano and paprika; pour over the meat and potatoes. Throw in a bay leaf.

Cook on high for 5-6 hours (low for 9-10). Stir and pull the bay leaf out.

Serve!

Sloppy Joes
Servings: 8

Prep Time: 20 min Cook time: 6 hrs

Ingredients

2 lbs ground beef
1 onion
1 can tomato sauce (8oz)
½ cup ketchup
¼ cup brown sugar
¼ cup flour
½ cup water
2 tbsp yellow mustard
1 tbsp Worcestershire sauce
1 tbsp apple cider vinegar
Chili powder, garlic powder, salt, pepper

For serving:

8 cheese slices
8 buns
2 tbsp olive oil
Salt or other seasonings you prefer best

Directions

Cook the meat and diced onion on the stove top, until meat is no longer pink.
Transfer the meat to the slow cooker (not the grease!).
Add in the remaining ingredients. Season, to taste. Stir well to mix.
Cook on low for 5-6 hours.
Serve on the hamburger buns (can be toasted) with a slice of cheese on top!

Chili Macaroni
Serving: 8

Prep Time: 10 min Cook time: 2 hrs 30 min

Ingredients

1 lbs ground beef
1 can chili beans (30 oz)
1 onion
2 cup beef broth
8 oz macaroni (pick your favorite shape!)
1 can crushed tomatoes (28 oz)
1 can diced tomatoes (15 oz)
Chili powder, cumin, salt, pepper
Cheddar cheese

Directions

Cook the meat on the stove top first, until no longer pink.
Transfer to the slow cooker. Add in beans, both kinds of tomatoes, diced onion, macaroni and broth. Season, to taste. Combine well.
Cook on low for 2 hours. If the macaroni are not tender enough, close and cook for extra 30 min.
Serve with some cheddar cheese on top!

Short Ribs in BBQ Sauce

Servings: 8
Prep Time: 20 min Cook Time: 8 hrs

Ingredients

5 lbs short beef ribs
1 onion
2 cup BBQ sauce
½ can beer
2 tbsp honey
2 tbsp Dijon mustard
Garlic powder, onion powder, pepper, salt

Directions

Sprinkle the ribs with salt, pepper, garlic and onion powders. Rub to coat good.
On the stove top brown up the outside of the ribs in the pan.
Cut up onion and lay out on the bottom of slow cooker.
Combine BBQ sauce, honey and mustard. Coat the ribs with the mix.
Lay the ribs on top of the onions. Pour beer on top.
Cook on low for 7-8 hours.
Serve!

Salisbury Steak

Servings: 6

Prep Time: 10 min Cook Time: 5 hrs

Ingredients

1 ½ lbs ground beef
1 egg yolk
onion
1/3 cup breadcrumbs
3 tbsp milk
1 garlic clove
Salt, pepper
1 can mushrooms (6 oz)
1 ½ cup beef broth
1 pkg brown gravy mix
2 tbsp ketchup
1 tsp Dijon mustard
Fresh parsley
4 tbsp water
2 tbsp corn starch

Directions

Combine beef, egg yolk, ½ diced onion, breadcrumbs, milk and minced garlic. Season, to taste. Make 6 patties. Brown up on both sides in the pan.

Drain the mushrooms and lay out on the bottom of the slow cooker with the remaining diced onion.

Mix broth, ketchup, mustard, parsley and gravy mix. Pour over the patties.

Cook on low for 5 hours.

When done, pull the patties out. Mix cornstarch and water and pour into the slow cooker. Stir well. Cook on high until the gravy thickens.

Serve a patty over rice or mashed potatoes with the gravy on top!

Bacon Pork Loin

Serving: 8
Prep Time: 10 min Cook Time: 4 hrs

Ingredients

- 3 lbs pork loin
- 4 garlic cloves
- 8 bacon slices
- 1/3 cup brown sugar
- 1 tbsp oil
- Salt, pepper

Directions

Trim the pork loin of excess fat. Mince garlic.
Rub the pork loin with oil and sprinkle with salt and pepper. Set in the slow cooker. Sprinkle brown sugar and minced garlic on top. Wrap the pork loin with bacon (as far as it will reach)
Cook on low for 4-5 hours.
Slice and serve!

Lasagna
Serving: 5

Prep Time: 10 min Cook Time: 10 min

Ingredients

½ lbs ground beef
½ lbs Italian sausage
1 can tomato sauce
1 can tomato paste
1 ¼ cup water
1 pkg lasagna noodles
1 ½ cup cottage cheese
½ cup parmesan
4 cups mozzarella
Italian seasoning, minced onion, parsley, garlic powder
salt, pepper

Directions

On the stove top cook beef and sausage. Sprinkle with minced onion. Season with Italian, parsley, garlic powder. Add salt and pepper if needed. Stir in Worcestershire sauce, tomato paste, tomato sauce, sugar and water. Simmer for 20 min.

Mix together Parmesan, mozzarella and cottage cheese.

Spread about a quarter of the meat sauce on the bottom of the slow cooker. Lay out the lasagna noodles. Spread the cheese mix. Repeat with 2 more layers. Sprinkle extra mozzarella on top.

Cook on low for 4-5 hours.

Serve!

Dr. Pepper Pulled Pork Serving: 6-8

Prep Time: 5 minCook Time: 4 hrs

Ingredients

1 pork shoulder roast
Onion
1 can Dr. Pepper
¾ cup BBQ sauce
Salt, pepper, garlic powder
Buns

Directions

Dice the onion and place to the bottom of the slow cooker.

Rub the roast with salt, pepper and garlic powder. Place the pork on top of the onion. Pour Dr. Pepper on top.
Cook on high for 4-5 hours (low for 7-8).
When done, shred the pork. Mix with BBQ sauce.
Serve on hamburger buns with a side of cole slaw!

Lo Mein
Servings: 6

Prep Time: 5 min Cook Time: 8 hrs 30 min

Ingredients

2 lbs boneless pork shoulder
3 cup broccoli
2 carrots
2 celery stalks
1 cup snow peas
1 can water chestnuts
1 lbs spaghetti noodles

Sauce:
1/3 cup soy sauce
2 tbsp brown sugar
1 tbsp oyster sauce
3 garlic cloves
1 tsp sesame oil
1 tbsp grated ginger

Directions

Place the pork to the slow cooker. Combine ingredients for the sauce and pour over the pork.

Cook on high for 3-4 hours (low for 7-8). When done, pull the pork out and shred (cut). Return to the slow cooker.

Cut up carrots and celery. Add in to the slow cooker along with broccoli, peas and chestnuts. Stir in. Cook for additional 30 min.

Cook spaghetti separately on the stove top.

Serve spaghetti with the meat, veggies and juices!

Pot RoastServing: 6

Prep Time: 10 minCook Time: 6 hrs

Ingredients

1 boneless chuck roast
1 lbs red potatoes
1 cup baby carrots
Onion
1 ½ beef broth
¼ cup Dijon mustard
Dried rosemary, thyme, garlic salt, pepper

Directions

Cut potatoes in quarters. Cut the roast in half. Dice the onion.

Mix seasoning in the mustard. Rub both parts of the roast, until well coated.

Lay out carrots and potatoes in the slow cooker. Place the roast on top, then top with onions and pour the broth in.

Cook on low for 6-8 hours, until the roast is tender.

Beef Ragu Serving 8

Prep Time: 10 min Cook Time: 2 hrs

Ingredients

1 ½ lbs flank steak
1 carrot
16 oz pasta
1 can crushed tomatoes (28 oz)
6 garlic cloves
1 tsp olive oil
¼ cup beef broth
Parmesan
2 bay leaves
Thyme, salt, pepper

Directions

Cut the steak in 4 pieces. Cut up the carrot.
Heat the oil in the pan and cook garlic until golden brown.
Season the meat and place in the slow cooker. Add in tomatoes, broth, cooked garlic, carrot. Sprinkle with thyme and throw in bay leafs.

Cook on high for 6 hours (low for 8-10). Pull out bay leaves. Shred the meat.

Cook the pasta on the stove top. Drain and stir in the slow cooker mix.

Serve with Parmesan on top!

Steak Fajitas
Servings: 6

Prep Time: 5 min Cook Time: 4 hrs

Ingredients

2 lbs beef
2 bell peppers
1 onion
1 jar salsa (20 oz)
2 tbsp fajita seasoning

Directions

Slice the beef. Cut up the peppers and clean out the seeds. Dice the onion.

Pour salsa to the bottom of the slow cooker. Add in the beef, onion and peppers. Sprinkle with seasoning. Mix well.

Cook on high for 3-4 hours (low for 6-8).

Serve with your favorite side or eat it as a whole meal!

Chicken

Chicken and Orzo Serving 4

Prep Time: 10 min Cook Time: 4 hrs

Ingredients

4 chicken breasts
3 cup chicken broth
1 cup orzo pasta
1 cup diced mushrooms
1 onion
1 tbsp olive oil
3 tbsp Italian seasoning
2 tsp minced garlic
Salt, pepper
Parmesan

Directions

On the stove top heat olive oil and fry the chicken until no longer pink on the outside. Sprinkle with seasoning. Place chicken in the slow cooker. Dice the onion and lay on top of the chicken. Add in mushrooms and garlic. Pour in the broth and melted butter.

Cook on high for 1-2 hours (low for 4). When time is up, stir in orzo pasta and cook for 30 more min (on high). Pull the chicken out and stir the pasta. Lay the chicken on top and sprinkle with parmesan. Cover and cook until cheese is melted (10-15 min).
Serve!

Hawaiian Chicken Serving 4

Prep Time: 15 min Cook Time: 6 hrs

Ingredients

4 chicken thighs
2 cup pineapple chunks
1 onion
1 red bell pepper
3 tbsp honey
2 tbsp soy sauce
½ cup brown sugar
2 garlic cloves
1 tbsp grated ginger
1 tbsp cornstarch + 1 tbsp water

Directions

In a pan cook chicken thighs on both sides until golden brown (no need to cook all the way through).
Place pineapple in the slow cooker. Dice the onion and add to the pineapples.
Mix honey, soy sauce, brown sugar, ginger and garlic. Stir in the slow cooker.
Lay out chicken thighs on top.
Cook on high for 3 hours (low for 5).

Cut and clean out the pepper. Mix water and cornstarch and add both to the slow cooker. Cook for 30 extra min.
Serve over rice!

Chicken and Mushrooms Serving 4

Prep Time: 10 min Cook Time: 6 hrs

Ingredients

4 chicken breasts
1 cup sliced mushrooms
1 cup chicken broth
½ cup water
¼ cup cornstarch
Salt, pepper, garlic powder

Directions

Place chicken breasts in the slow cooker. Put the mushrooms on top. Pour in chicken broth.
Cook for 5 hours on high.
Pull chicken out and add in water and cornstarch. Mix well. Put the chicken back in. Cook for 30 extra min, to let the gravy thicken.
Serve over mashed potatoes or noodles!

Spicy Chicken and Rice

Serving 8

Prep Time: 5 min Cook Time: 4 hrs 30 min

Ingredients

4 chicken breasts
1 can tomatoes (14oz)
1 can enchilada sauce
1 can black beans
4 cups cooked rice
Garlic powder, smoked paprika, cumin, chipotle pepper, salt
¾ cup sharp cheddar
¾ cup pepper jack cheese
cilantro

Directions

Put chicken breasts to the bottom of the slow cooker.
Mix tomatoes with enchilada sauce. Sprinkle with seasoning, to taste. Stir.
Pour the mixture over the chicken.
Cook on low for 4 hours.
When time is up, pull out chicken and shred. Transfer back to the slow cooker. Add in cooked rice, beans and cheese. Stir well. Cook for additional 30 min.
Serve with some chopped cilantro on top!

Chicken Rice Casserole Serving 6

Prep Time: 10 min Cook Time: 6 hrs

Ingredients

1 lbs chicken breasts
1 cup brown rice
1 onion
2 ¾ cup chicken broth
1 lbs steamed broccoli
½ plain yogurt
1 cup Parmesan
1 cup cheddar
Garlic powder, dried thyme, salt, pepper

Directions

Dice the onion and mix with rice. Spread out on the bottom of the slow cooker. Pour in chicken broth and lay the chicken breasts on top.

Cook on high for 3 hours (low for 6-7), until rice is tender.

Pull the chicken out and cut into small pieces. Stir in yogurt, parmesan, cheddar and cut up chicken. Add in broccoli right before serving!

Chicken Tacos Serving 8

Prep Time: 5 min Cook Time: 4 hrs

Ingredients

2 lbs chicken breasts
1 jar salsa (16 oz)
1 pkg taco seasoning
Juice from 2 limes
1/3 cup cut up cilantro
Taco shells
Lettuce, tomatoes, cheese and sour cream for serving

Directions

Place chicken breasts in the slow cooker. Pour salsa on top, sprinkle with cilantro and lime juice.
Cook on high for 4 hours (low for 6-7).
When chicken is done, pull it out and shred. If the chicken is too dry use leftover juice from the slow cooker to mix in with the shredded chicken.
Use your favorite toppings (like lettuce, tomatoes and cheese) to make tacos. Serve with sour cream!

Sweet Chili Drumsticks Serving 6

Prep Time: 10 min + 3 hrs Cook Time: 4 hrs

Ingredients

4 lbs chicken drumsticks
2/3 cup soy sauce
2/3 cup sweet chili sauce
1 tbsp fish sauce
Minced ginger root
Fresh cilantro
Sesame seeds

Directions

Combine soy sauce, chili sauce and fish sauce in a Ziploc bag. Add in minced ginger and drumsticks. Seal the bag and give it good shake. Make sure all of the drumsticks are fully covered. Let si tin the fridge for 3 hours to marinate.

When the time is up, pull the chicken out of the bag and place in the slow cooker. Dump the sauce from the bag on top of the chicken.

Cook on high for 4 hours (low for 6).

When done, pull drumsticks out and lay them out on a baking sheet. Brush with leftover sauce from the slow cooker and broil for 3 min. Flip the drumsticks over and repeat.

Sprinkle with sesame seeds and chopped cilantro. Serve with rice!

Jambalaya Serving 6

Prep Time: 10 min Cook Time: 8 hrs

Ingredients

2 chicken breasts
½ lbs uncooked shrimp
1 pkg andouline sausage
3 bell peppers (green, yellow, orange)
1 onion
3 jalapenos
1 ½ cup white rice
2 cup chicken broth
1 can crushed tomatoes (30 oz)
3 tbsp Cajun seasoning
1 tbsp minced garlic
Salt, pepper

Directions

Slice sausage, cut up chicken and peel the tails off the shrimp.
Cut up and clean out the seeds from peppers and jalapenos.

Place all of the ingredients, besides rice and shrimp, in the slow cooker. Season, to taste. Stir well.

Cook on low for 3-4 hours. Add in rice and cook for additional hour (2 hours if the rice is not tender enough).

Finally, add shrimp and cook for another 20 min. Stir well.

Serve while it's hot!

Cashew Chicken Serving 4

Prep Time: 15 min Cook Time: 4 hrs

Ingredients

- 2 lbs chicken breasts
- 1 cup cashews
- 3 tbsp cornstarch
- 1 tbsp oil
- ½ cup soy sauce
- 4 tbsp ketchup
- 4 tbsp rice vinegar
- 2 tbsp brown sugar
- 2 tbsp sweet chili sauce
- 1 tsp grated ginger
- ½ tsp red pepper flakes
- 2 garlic cloves

Directions

Mix cornstarch and pepper in a Ziploc bag. Cut the chicken in small pieces and add to the bag. Seal and shake to coat all the pieces well.
Brown up chicken in the pan, on the stove top (for about 2 min). Transfer chicken to the slow cooker.
Mix together soy sauce, ketchup, vinegar, chili sauce garlic, ginger and pepper flakes.
Put cashews in with the chicken and pour the sauce mix on top.
Cook on low for 3-4 hours.
Serve over rice!

Chicken in Creamy Sauce Serving 4

Prep Time: 10 minCook Time: 4 hrs

Ingredients

6 chicken breasts
½ cup sun dried tomatoes
¼ cup flour
4 tbsp olive oil
1 cup heavy cream
2 cup chicken stock
2 tbsp basil
Salt, pepper

Directions

Preheat oil in the pan on the stove top. Roll chicken in flour, season with salt and pepper. Fry on both sides for 2 min.
Transfer to the slow cooker. Add in chicken stock, tomatoes and basil.
Cook on low for 4-5 hours.
Pull chicken out and pour in heavy cream. Mix well and lay chicken on top. Cook for additional 5-10 min.
Serve over noodles!

Chicken Alfredo Serving 6

Prep Time: 10 min Cook Time: 6 hrs

Ingredients

- 1 ½ lbs chicken breasts
- 3 ½ cups Alfredo sauce
- 4 cup cooked cheese tortellini
- 1 tsp minced garlic
- Pepper, to taste

Directions

Put frozen chicken breasts in the slow cooker and dump 2 ½ cups of Alfredo sauce on top.

Cook on high for 6-8 hours.

Pull the chicken out and cut up on smaller pieces (or shred).

Put chicken back in the slow cooker, along with tortellini, garlic and remaining sauce. Stir well.

Cook for additional 15 min on high.

Serve while hot!

Whole Chicken Serving 2

Prep Time: 5 min Cook Time: 6 hours

Ingredients

1 whole chicken (small enough to fit in your Slow cooker!)
1 onion
1 garlic head
Rosemary, thyme, paprika, lemon pepper, salt, pepper
1 tbsp olive oil

Directions

Make sure to pull everything from inside the chicken.
Brush the chicken with olive oil.
Mix the seasonings and rub on the chicken.
Cut the onion in quarters and lay on the bottom of the slow cooker. Peel the garlic and separate and cloves. Throw them in between the onion. Set the chicken on top.
Cook on low for 6-8 hours.
Cut it up and serve with your favorite side!

Lettuce Wraps Serving 6

Prep Time: 15 min Cook Time: 3 hrs

Ingredients

- 2 lbs ground chicken
- 1 red bell pepper
- ½ diced onion
- 1 can water chestnuts (8 oz)
- 1 ½ cup cooked rice
- 3 garlic cloves
- ½ hoisin sauce
- 2 tbsp soy sauce
- 2 Iceberg lettuce heads
- 3 green onions

Directions

Cook chicken and garlic in the pan, until chicken is no longer pink. Drain the grease.
Cut and clean out bell pepper.
Transfer to the slow cooker; add in pepper, onion, hoisin sauce and soy sauce. Season, with salt and pepper.
 Cook on low for 2 hours.
When chicken is tender stir in rice, slices green onion, chestnuts and cook for additional 5 min.

Lay out lettuce leaves on the plate and fill with chicken mix. Serve!

Chicken Stew Serving: 4

Prep Time: 15 min Cook Time: 6 hrs

Ingredients

1 ½ lbs chicken breasts
1 onion
1 ½ lbs red potatoes
1 pkg baby carrots
½ cup water
½ cup milk + 3 tbsp cornstarch
Seasonings, to taste, parsley flakes

Directions

Cut up chicken to medium size pieces. Cut onion and potatoes.
Put chicken and veggies in the slow cooker. Season to taste and mix, to get everything covered.
Cook on low for 6 hours.
Mix cornstarch with milk; stir in the slow cooker. Cook on high for 15 extra min.
Serve!

Easy Chicken Dinner Serving 4

Prep Time: 15 min Cook Time: 4 hrs

Ingredients

2 lbs chicken breast
½ lbs fresh green beans
1 lbs baby red potatoes (can be cut in halves or quarters)
1/3 cup fresh lemon juice
¼ cup olive oil
2 garlic cloves
Dried oregano, onion powder, garlic powder, salt, pepper

Directions

Place the chicken breasts in the middles and lay out green beans on one side and potatoes on the other.
Whisk olive oil with lemon juice and seasonings. Add in minced garlic. Pour over chicken, green beans and potatoes.
Cook on high for 4 hours.
Super easy dump and go dinner is ready to be served!

Chicken Stroganoff
Serving 4

Prep Time: 5 min Cook Time: 5 hrs

Ingredients

4 chicken breasts
1 can sliced mushrooms (8 oz)
1 pkg cream cheese (8 oz)
1 can cream of chicken soup (10 oz)
1 tbsp butter
1 pkg dry onion soup mix (1 ¼ oz)
Salt, pepper

Directions

Cut up chicken in bite sized pieces. Grease the bottom of the slow cooker with butter. Lay out chicken and put the mushrooms (drained!) on top. Season, to taste.

Mix cream cheese, onion soup mix and chicken soup until smooth. Pour on top of chicken and mushrooms and spread to get everything covered.

Cook on high for 3-4 hours (low for 4-6).

Serve over noodles!

Chicken Noodle Casserole Serving 6

Prep Time: 10 min Cook Time: 4 hrs 30 min

Ingredients

2 chicken breasts
1 can crushed tomatoes
12 oz pasta (not cooked)
¼ cup water
2 cup mozzarella
Parmesan
2 tbsp olive oil
Salt, pepper, dried basil, minced garlic

Directions

Lay chicken in the slow cooker and add crushed tomatoes and water. Season, to taste.
Cook on high for 4 hours (low for 8).
Pull the chicken out and shred.
Transfer back into the slow cooker and add pasta. Stir to get paste fully covered in the liquids.
Cook for additional 20 min on high.
Stir in Parmesan and sprinkle with mozzarella. Cook on low for another 10 min (or until cheese melts).
Sprinkle with extra Parmesan and serve!

Lemon Garlic Chicken

Serving 6

Prep Time: 10 min   Cook Time: 5 hrs

Ingredients

- 2 lbs chicken breasts
- 2 tbsp butter
- ¼ cup water
- 3 tbsp fresh lemon juice
- 2 minced garlic cloves
- 1 tbsp chicken bouillon
- Dried oregano, salt, pepper, parsley flakes

Directions

Sprinkle the seasonings over chicken and rub to coat well.

Preheat butter in the pan and cook chicken until no longer pink on the outside. Leave the grease and transfer chicken to the slow cooker.

Pour water, lemon juice and add bouillon to the pan with the chicken grease. Bring to a boil. Pour into the slow cooker.

Cook on low for 4-5 hours. Sprinkle with parsley and baste the chicken breasts. Cook for additional 20 min on high.

Serve with rice!

Sesame Chicken
Serving 4

Prep Time: 15 min
Cook Time: 10 min + 2 hrs

Ingredients

- 1/2lbs chicken breasts
- ¼ cup soy sauce
- ½ cup honey
- 2 tbsp ketchup
- 1 tbsp oil
- dried onion, garlic powder, sesame seeds
- 2 tbsp cornstarch +3 tbsp water

Directions

Put chicken breast in the slow cooker.
Mix soy sauce, honey, ketchup, oil, garlic and onion. Pour on top on chicken.
Cook on high for 2 ½ hours (low for 3-4).
Pull out chicken and cut into small pieces.
Mix cornstarch with water, until smooth and stir into the slow cooker.
Cook on high for 10 min, until the sauce thickens.
Transfer chicken back into the slow cooker. Cook for another 10 min on low.
Sprinkle with sesame seeds and serve over rice!

Chicken Sandwiches Serving 6

Prep Time: 5 min Cook Time: 6 hrs 15 min

Ingredients

4 chicken breasts
1 lbs bacon
1 pkg cream cheese (8 oz)
1 cup mayo
2 cups cheddar cheese
½ cup cut up green onions
1 pkg ranch dressing mix
6 Buns

Directions

Put chicken breasts in the slow cooker and sprinkle with ranch mix. Spread cream cheese on top.
Cook on low for 6 hours.
Pull the chicken out and shred.
Cook bacon and chop into small pieces.
Return chicken to the slow cooker, along with bacon and mayo. Mix well. Sprinkle with cheese.
Cook for 15 more min.
Top with green onions.
Serve on the buns!

Veggies/Sides

Loaded Potatoes Serving 6

Prep Time: 15 min Cook Time: 5 hrs

Ingredients

1 lbs baby potatoes
3 cup cheddar
8 bacon slices
2 garlic cloves
¼ cup cut green onions
Cooking spray
Paprika, salt, pepper
Sour cream for serving

Directions

Spray slow cooker with cooking spray (or grease with some olive oil). You can also use foil for an easy clean up.
Cut potatoes in quarters, cooked and chop bacon and cut garlic cloves in slices (!!).
Load potatoes in the slow cooker, top half the cheese, some of the bacon, green onions and garlic.
Cook on high for 4-5 hours (poke potatoes with a fork to check).
Sprinkle remaining cheese and bacon on top and cook for another 20 min (just until cheese melts).

Serve with a side of sour cream!

Caramelized Onions Serving size 3 cups

Prep Time: 10 min Cook Time: 12 hrs

Ingredients

3-4 lbs white onions
3 tbsp butter
Salt, pepper

Directions

Cut the onions in thin slices. Load in the slow cooker. Melt the butter and drizzle over the onions. Stir to get all the onions covered with butter.

Cook on low for 8-10 hours. Season and stir.

Once the onions are really juicy, open the lid, no more than an inch, and continue cooking for 2-4 hours.

Once the onions are brown and thick, that means they are done!

Serve with your favorite dish!

Whole Cauliflower Serving 6-8

Prep Time: 5 min Cook Time: 6 hrs

Ingredients

Whole cauliflower
1 cup vegetable broth
1 tbsp ranch dressing mix
3 tbsp ranch dressing

Directions

Remove the green leaves and trim the bottom, to fit in the slow cooker.

Rub seasonings on the outside of the cauliflower. Pour the broth in the slow cooker and set in cauliflower.

Cook on high for 4 hours (low for 6 hours).

Once done, brush the outside with ranch dressing and broil in the oven until golden brown (5 min).

Cut into wedges and serve!

Butternut squash Serving 8

Prep Time: 20 min Cook Time: 3 hrs

Ingredients

4-pound butternut squash
½ cup butter
¾ cup brown sugar
1 tsp cinnamon, a pinch ground cloves and nutmeg

Directions

Peel and clean out the squash. Cut into squares.
Load in the slow cooker. Sprinkle with cinnamon, nutmeg and cloves. Cut up butter on top of the squash. Cook on high for 3 hours.
Serve and enjoy!

Spinach Lasagna Serving 6-8

Prep Time: 20 min Cook Time: 4 hrs

Ingredients

2 cup frozen spinach
1 pkg lasagna noodles
2 jars Alfredo sauce
2 cups Italian cheese blend
½ cup Parmesan

Directions

Prepare spinach and let cool. Squeeze out excess liquid. Mix Alfredo sauce with ½ cup Italian cheese blend.

Grease the slow cooker with cooking spray. Spread ¼ of sauce mix on the bottom, layer noodles on top, then spinach and cheese. Continue, until you make 3 layers. Finish with noodles and spread remaining sauce on top. Sprinkle with leftover cheese and parmesan.

Cook on low for 3-4 hours (if the noodles are not tender enough add extra 30min).

Cut up in slices and serve hot with extra parmesan on top!

Green Beans with Ham

Serving 6

Prep Time: 15 min Cook Time: 4 hrs

Ingredients

1 lbs green beans (fresh)
2 cups cooked ham
1 onion
3 ½ cup chicken broth
1 tbsp cider vinegar
pepper

Directions

Trim green beans, dice ham. Slice onion.
Load everything in the slow cooker; pour broth and vinegar over top. Season, to taste.
Cook on high for 4 hours.
Ready to serve!

Sweet Potatoes Serving 8

Prep Time: 15 min Cook Time: 4 hrs 10 min

Ingredients

5 lbs sweet potatoes
½ cup chicken stock
¼ cup brown sugar
4 tbsp butter
2 tsp cinnamon
½ tsp nutmeg
1 tsp salt
2 cup mini marshmallows

Directions

Peel and cube potatoes.
Grease the slow cooker and put in potatoes. Add in brown sugar and pour in the stock.
Cook on high for 4 hours, stirring every hour.
Add in butter and seasoning. Mix well and let sit for 5 min.
Mash the potatoes (or use a blender). Lay out marshmallow to cover the top. Cook for additional 10 min on high, until marshmallows are melted.
Serve!

Pizza Bake Serving 4

Prep Time: 10 min Cook Time: 2 hrs

Ingredients

1 can biscuits
1 cup pizza sauce
2 cups Mozzarella
1 cup pepperoni
3 tsp Italian seasoning
Parmesan

Directions

I recommend using an insert for the slow cooker to make pulling pizza out easier (or foil)

Cut up biscuits and half of the pepperoni in quarters. Put in a bowl and season. Mix to get all of biscuits nicely covered.

Lay out biscuits and pepperoni mix in the slow cooker. Spread pizza sauce over the top and add in remaining pepperoni. Sprinkle with cheese. Cook on high for 1-2 hours. When the biscuits are golden brown at the edge, pull the pizza out.

Sprinkle with some parmesan and serve!

Ranch Mushrooms Serving 4

Prep Time: 10 min Cook Time: 2 hrs

Ingredients

1 lbs fresh mushrooms
1 pkg ranch dressing mix
1 stick butter (1/2 cup)

Directions

Melt the butter and stir in ranch mix.
Wipe off the mushrooms with a paper towel (do not wash!).
Load the mushrooms in the slow cooker and pour butter mix over them.
Cook on high for 1-2 hours (low 3-4).
Remove the lid and let the excess liquids to evaporate.
Serve!

Creamed Spinach Serving 5

Prep Time: 5 min Cook Time: 8 hrs

Ingredients

36 oz frozen spinach
1 stick butter (1/2 cup)
1 onion
4 garlic cloves
2 ¾ cup milk
¼ cup flour
Nutmeg, cayenne pepper, white pepper, salt
1 cup parmesan

Directions

Melt the butter in the pan. Dice onion and mince garlic. Add to the pan. Sauté until onion is soft (5 min). Add in flour and stir well until all the chunks are gone.

Transfer the mix to the slow cooker. Add in frozen spinach, milk and seasonings.

Cook on high for 8-10 hours (don't forget to stir every couple hours!).

Stir in parmesan before serving!

Brown Rice and Mushrooms Serving 4

Prep Time: 10 min Cook Time: 3 hrs

Ingredients

2 cup brown rice
8 oz sliced mushrooms
2 tbsp butter
4 cups beef froth
Thyme, oregano, salt, pepper
lbs fresh mushrooms
1 pkg ranch dressing mix
1 stick butter (1/2 cup)
Cheese of your choice

Directions

Melt the butter in the pan on the stove top. Sauté rice until it is lightly toasted. Transfer to the slow cooker. Add in mushrooms and pour broth over top. Sprinkle with seasonings. Stir.

Cook on high for 2-3 hours (if rice is not cooked through, add ½ cup of broth or water and cook for additional 30 min).

Sprinkle with cheese before serving!

Baked Beans Serving 6

Prep Time: 20 min Cook Time: 4 hrs 20 min

Ingredients

3 cans pork and beans (not drained)
1 can nothern beans
1 can navy beans
6 bacon pieces
1 onion
¾ cup ketchup
¼ cup brown sugar
¼ cup molasses
2 tbsp yellow mustard
1 tbsp Worcestershire sauce
Garlic powder, cayenne pepper, salt, pepper

Directions

Cook bacon in the pan on the stove top. Lay out on the paper towel to catch excess grease. Save 1 tbsp of bacon grease from the pan. Dice the onion. And soften up in bacon grease.

Drain and rinse northern and navy beans.

Load the slow cooker with beans and onion. Add in ketchup, brown sugar, molasses, mustard and Worcestershire sauce. Season, to taste.

Cook on low for 4 hours. Remove the slid and cook on high for 20 min to thicken.

Chop bacon and stir in.

Serve!

Warm Brussels Sprouts Salad Serving 8

Prep Time: 20 min Cook Time: 2 hrs 30 min

Ingredients

4 cups Brussels sprouts
4 cups butternut squash
1 red onion
1 cup fresh cranberries
½ cup pecans

Sauce:
¼ cup maple syrup
2 tbsp apple cider vinegar
Cinnamon, nutmeg, salt

Directions

Load squash, Brussels sprouts and cut up onion in the slow cooker.

Cook on high for 2 hours (if squash is not tender enough add extra 30 min).

Add cranberries and cook for additional 5 min.

Sauce:

Mix maple syrup and vinegar with seasonings in a small pot on the stove top. Bring to a boil and reduce heat to low. Simmer for 5 min, until it thickens.

Pour over veggies and sprinkle with pecans. Ready to serve!

Corn on the Cob Serving 2

Prep Time: 5 min Cook Time: 2 hrs

Ingredients

4 corn ears
1 small onion
1 can coconut milk (15 oz)
2 tbsp butter
1 minced garlic clove
Pepper, salt, thyme

Directions

Load the slow cooker with corn (depending on the size of your slow cooker you may need to cut corn ears in half), coconut milk, garlic and diced onion. Season, to taste.
Cook on high for 2 hours.
Pull out corn and drain extra liquids.
Serve with extra butter and seasoning of your choice!

Mashed Potatoes Serving 8

Prep Time: 20 min Cook Time: 4 hrs

Ingredients

5 lbs potatoes
1 cup chicken broth
4 garlic cloves
1/3 cup butter
2/3 cup sour cream
½ cup milk (hot!)
½ cup Parmesan
Salt, pepper

Directions

Peel and dice potatoes. Load in the slow cooker along with broth, butter and minced garlic. Season, to taste. Mix well.
Cook on high for 4 hours (low for 7-8).
Mash potatoes; gradually stir in milk and sour cream, until nice and smooth. Add in parmesan.
Serve warm!

Butter Carrots Serving 4

Prep Time: 10 min Cook Time: 3 hrs

Ingredients

2 lbs carrots
1 onion
¼ cup butter
¼ cup fresh lemon juice
1 tbsp lemon zest
1 tbsp fresh chopped thyme
2 tbsp brown sugar
Salt, pepper

Directions

Mince garlic; dice the onion. Cut up carrots to look like thick fries, load in the slow cooker along with the onion.

Mix garlic, lemon juice and zest and thyme. Pour over carrots. Season, to taste.

Cook on high for 3 hours. Stir once or twice.

If the carrots are too tart for your taste, feel free to add the brown sugar.

Serve with some extra thyme on top!

Garlic and Herb Mushrooms Serving 4

Prep Time: 5 min Cook Time: 3 hrs

Ingredients

1 ½ lbs mushrooms
2 tbsp butter
4 garlic cloves
½ cup vegetable broth
¼ cup half and half
½ cup parmesan
Dried oregano, thyme, parsley

Directions

Melt butter and mix with oregano, thyme and minced garlic. Load mushrooms in the slow cooker, pour broth and butter mix on top. Toss to mix.
Cook on high for 1-2 hours (low for 2-3). Mix in half and half and parmesan, stir.
Serve with some parsley on top!

Scalloped Potatoes Serving 8

Prep Time: 20 min Cook Time: 5 hrs 20 min

Ingredients

2 lbs russet potatoes
1 ½ cup heavy cream
3 garlic cloves
1 cup swiss cheese
¼ cup parmesan
Salt, pepper, thyme

Directions

Peel and slice potatoes.
Mix heavy cream, thyme, nutmeg and minced garlic in a pan. Warm up at medium heat.
Layer potatoes on the bottom of your slow cooker (the might overlap and I's fine). Pour some of the heavy cream mix and sprinkle with cheese. Repeat until potatoes and cream are gone.
Cook on high for 4-5 hours.
When done, sprinkle with parmesan and let sit for 5 extra min until cheese is melted.
Open the lid and let sit for 15 min, so the sauce can thicken.
Sprinkle with extra parmesan and serve!

Creamed Corn Serving 6

Prep Time: 10 min Cook Time: 2 hrs

Ingredients

5 can corn kernels (15 oz)
8 bacon slices
1 cup milk
1 pkg cream cheese (8 oz)
1 stick butter (1/2 cup)
1 tbsp sugar
Salt, pepper

Directions

Chop bacon into small pieces.
Drain corn and dump in the slow cooker. Add in milk, sugar and half of the bacon. Season, to taste. Stir in cream cheese and butter.
Cook on high for 2 hours, stirring halfway through.
Sprinkle with remaining bacon and serve!

White Rice Serving 4

Prep Time: 5 min Cook Time: 2 hrs

Ingredients

1 cup rice
2 cup water
*to make more rice simply double both water and rice
Seasoning, to taste

Directions

Load rice and water in the slow cooker. Season, to taste. Stir.

Cook on high for 2-3 hours. If the rice is not tender enough, add 30 more min at a time, until nice and fluffy.

Serve with meat, chicken or your favorite veggies!

Mashed Cauliflower Serving 6

Prep Time: 15 min Cook Time: 3 hrs

Ingredients

1 cauliflower head
1 cup vegetable broth
5 cups water
3 tbsp butter
6 garlic cloves
Herbs: rosemary, thyme, parsley

Directions

Trim the green leaves off the cauliflower and cut into florets. Load in the slow cooker. Add in garlic cloves; pour in broth and then enough water to cover cauliflower.
Cook on high for 3 hours (low for 6 hours).
Drain the liquids and place cauliflower back into the slow cooker. Add butter and mash. Season with herbs and salt/pepper, to taste. Give it a good stir and keep on low to warm through.
Serve!

Soups

Hearty Vegetable Serving 4

Prep Time: 15 min Cook Time: 8 hrs

Ingredients

1 onion
2 carrots
2 celery stalks
2 garlic cloves
6 cup vegetable broth
1 can crushed tomatoes
1/3 cup split peas
1/3 cup lentils
1/3 cup barley
2 tbsp olive oil
Oregano, parsley, salt, pepper

Directions

Cut and slice veggies to approximately the same size. Mince garlic.
Preheat oil in the pan on the stove top. Sauté onion and garlic until soft.

Load the veggies in the slow cooker along with onion mix, peas, barley and lentils. Pour the broth in. Season, to taste.

Cook on low for 8 hours. Give it a stir once in a while; adjust the seasonings, if needed.

Let rest for 5 min before serving!

Toscana Soup Serving 6

Prep Time: 10 min Cook Time: 4 hrs

Ingredients

- 1 lbs ground hot italian sausage
- 4 russet potatoes
- 1 onion
- 3 garlic cloves
- ½ pc bunch kale
- Chicken stock (32 oz)
- 1 cup heavy cream
- 2 tbsp flour
- Salt, pepper, red pepper flakes

Directions

Dice onion and cube potatoes. Mince garlic and tear kale into bite sized pieces.

Brown sausage in the pan, add garlic in the last minute. Drain the grease and transfer to the slow cooker. Add in potatoes and onion, pour in chicken stock and add water (enough to cover potatoes).

Cook on high for 3-4 hours (low for 5-6).

Mix flour and heavy cream and stir into the soup, add in kale. Mix and cook for 30 extra min on high.

Once the soup thickens it is ready to be served!

MinestroneServing 6-8

Prep Time: 10 minCook Time: 4 hrs 25 min

Ingredients

1 cup diced carrots
1 cup diced celery
1 cup diced onion
1 can kidney beans (15oz)
1 can northern beans (15 oz)
1 cup diced zucchini
1 cup pasta
1 cup frozen green beans
2 cups diced spinach
2 cans diced tomatoes
2 tbsp tomato paste
3 cups vegetable stock

2 cups water
4 garlic cloves
¼ cup sun dried tomato pesto
Oregano, rosemary, salt, pepper, 2 bay leaves

Directions

Load the slow cooker with tomatoes, tomato paste, vegetable stock, water, carrots, celery, onion and garlic. Season, to taste. Throw in bay leaves.
Cook on high for 3-4 hours (low 6-8).
Drain the beans and stir in the soup. Add in zucchini and pasta. Cook for 20 extra min. When the pasta is tender, mix in green beans and spinach, and keep on low for 10 min.
Serve with parmesan sprinkled on top!

Lasagna Soup

Serving 6-8

Prep Time: 15 min Cook Time: 4 hrs

Ingredients

1 lbs ground Italian sausage
1 onion
3 carrots
4 garlic cloves
1 can tomato sauce (15 oz)
2 cans diced tomatoes (14.5 oz)
1 can sliced mushrooms (8 oz)
1 cup rotini pasta
Dried basil, Italian seasoning, salt, pepper
2 cups mozzarella cheese

Directions

Dice onion and carrots. Mince garlic.
Cook sausage, carrots and onion in the pan. Cook until sausage is brown.
Transfer to the slow cooker, along with diced tomatoes (with the juice), tomato sauce, mushrooms and water. Season, to taste, and stir.
Cook on high for 4 hours (low for 8 hours).
In the last 10 min stir in pasta. Cook until pasta is soft.
Serve with some mozzarella on top!

Creamy Tortellini Soup Serving 8

Prep Time: 15 min Cook Time: 5 hrs 5 min

Ingredients

1 lbs ground sausage
1 onion
2 carrots
2 celery stalks
4 garlic cloves
4 cups beef broth
¼ cup cornstarch mixed with ¼ water
3 can half and hald (12 oz)
1 pkg three cheese tortellini
5 cups fresh spinach
1 cup milk
2 bouillon cubes
Salt, pepper, itallian seasoning

Directions

Dice the onion and carrots, cut up celery.
Cook sausage with onion, until nice and brown. Transfer to the slow cooker. Add in carrots, celery, garlic and broth. Season, to taste. Sprinkle with the bouillon cube.

Cook on high for 4 hours (low for 7). Skim extra fat from the top. Add in half and half, cornstarch mix and tortellini. Mix well.

Cook on high for 45 more min.

Finally, add spinach and stir well, so that the spinach is covered in the soup. Cook for additional 10 min.

Pour in milk, to get the consistency you like, season, if needed.

Serve!

Bacon Corn Chowder Serving 8

Prep Time: 15 min Cook Time: 3 hrs 30 min

Ingredients

1 lbs red potatoes
½ cup diced onion
2 bags frozen corn kernels (12 oz ea.)
2 cup chicken broth
2 cup half and half
2 tbsp cornstarch
½ lbs bacon (cooked)

Directions

Dice potatoes, load in the slow cooker. Add in onion, corn and broth. Season, to taste.

Cook on high for 3-4 hours.
Whisk half and half with cornstarch. Mix in the soup.
Crumble bacon and stir in.
Cook for additional 10 min.
Serve!

Chicken Rice Soup Serving 8

Prep Time: 15 min Cook Time: 4 hrs

Ingredients

3 chicken breasts
1 cup brown rice
1 onion
3 carrots
3 celery stalks
3 garlic cloves
9 cups chicken broth
2 tbsp butter
Parsley, rosemary, thyme, salt, pepper

Directions

Dice onion, carrots, celery and mince garlic. Cube chicken.
Transfer to the slow cooker. Pour in the broth. Add butter and season, to taste.
Cook on low for 4 hours. After 2 hours, add in rice, stir and continue cooking.
Serve with some toasted bread!

Chicken Fajita Soup Serving 4

Prep Time: 10 min Cook Time: 4 hrs

Ingredients

1 lbs chicken breasts
2 cans cream of chicken
1 cup salsa
1 ½ cup water
1 can black beans (15 oz)
2 cup frozen corn
1 cup cheddar cheese
1 tbsp butter
Ground cumin, dried cilantro, salt, pepper

Directions

Grease the slow cooker with butter, lay out chicken.
Mix chicken soup with salsa, corn, drained beans, water and seasonings. Pour over chicken.
Cook on low for 4-6 hours.
Pull out chicken and shred. Return to the slow cooker. Add in cheese, mix and continue cooking until cheese is melted (15 min).
Serve with diced avocado, tomatoes, sour cream or just extra cheese!

French Onion Soup Serving 8

Prep Time: 20 min Cook Time: 6 hrs

Ingredients

3 onions
3 tbsp butter
2 tbsp brown sugar
64 oz beef broth
1 tbsp Worcestershire sauce
1 garlic clove
bay leaf
1 cup swiss
¼ cup parmesan
dried thyme

Directions

Slice onion and cook in the pan with brown sugar and butter. Once onions caramelize, transfer them to the slow cooker. Add in broth, sauce, minced garlic clove, bay leaf and thyme. Stir.
Cook on low for 6-8 hours.
Pull out bay leaf. Serve with cheese mix on top and grilled (toasted bread)!

Tomato Basil Soup Serving 8

Prep Time: 15 min Cook Time: 8 hrs

Ingredients

1 onion
2 carrots
1 can tomato sauce
2 cans diced tomatoes
4 garlic cloves
1 tbsp sugar
4 cup vegetable broth
2 tbsp balsamic vinegar
2 cups half and half
2 tbsp butter
Salt ,pepper, basil, Italian seasoning
Bay leaf
Fresh basil and parmesan for serving

Directions

Dice onion and carrots, mince garlic. Preheat butter in the pan and cook onion and carrots until soft. Transfer to the slow cooker.
Add in tomatoes and tomato sauce, garlic, broth, vinegar, bay leaf and seasonings.
Cook on high 3-4 hours (low for 6-8).

Pull out bay leaf and add in basil. Blend the soup until smooth. Stir in half and half, ½ cup at a time. Depending on your taste add 1 cup or 2.
Serve with grilled cheese (of course!)!

ChiliServing 6

Prep Time: 10 minCook Time: 6 hrs
Ingredients

2 lbs ground beef
1 onion
3 garlic cloves
2 can diced tomatoes (14.5 oz)
3 can tomato sauce(8 oz)
½ cup beef broth
1 can red kidney beans
1 can light kidney beans
Salt, pepper, ground cumin, paprika, ground coriander, chili powder
2 tsp cocoa powder
Cheese and sour cream for serving

Directions

Cook onion and garlic in the pan with some oil, until soft. Transfer to the slow cooker.

Brown up the beef; drain all but 2 tbsp of grease and put in the slow cooker along with the beef.

Stir in diced tomatoes and paste, broth, minced garlic and diced onion. Season, to taste. Mix in cocoa powder.

Cook on low for 5-6 hours.

Drain the beans and stir in the soup. Cook for 10 extra min.

Serve with cheese and sour cream on top!

Chicken Noodle Serving 8

Prep Time: 15 min Cook Time: 8 hrs 30 min

Ingredients

- 1 ½ lbs chicken breasts
- 8 cup chicken stock
- 1 onion
- 3 carrots
- 3 celery stalks
- 8 oz spaghetti noodles
- Juice from 1 lemon
- Salt, pepper, dried thyme and rosemary
- 2 bay leaves
- Fresh parsley for serving

Directions

Dice onion, carrots and celery; mince garlic.
Cut up chicken in cubes and load in the slow cooker, add in stock, garlic, onion, carrots and celery. Season, to taste. Drop in two bay leaves.
Cook on low for 6-8 hours.
Break noodles in third and stir into the soup. Cook for 30 extra min.
Squeeze in lemon juice and stir.
Serve with some chopped parsley on top!

Ham and White Bean Soup Serving 10

Prep Time: 10 min Cook Time: 4 hrs

Ingredients

1 leftover ham bone
3 cups diced ham
1 onion
3 carrots
2 celery stalks
3 cans white cannellini beans
4 cups vegetable stock

Dried thyme and rosemary, salt, pepper
2 bay leaves
Fresh parsley for serving

Directions

Brown the ham bone in the slow cooker on all sides.
Dice carrots, onion and celery.
Load the slow cooker with diced ham, vegetables and drained beans. Pour in stock and stir. Season, to taste.
Cook on high for 3-4 hours (low for 6-8).
Pull out the bone and throw it out.
Serve with some chopped parsley on top!

White Chili Serving 6

Prep Time: 5 min Cook Time: 5 hrs

Ingredients

1 lbs chicken breasts
1 onion
24 oz chicken broth
2 cans northern beans (15 oz ea)
2 cans diced green chilies (4 oz ea)
1 can whole kernel corn (15 oz)
¼ cup half and half
4 oz cream cheese
Salt, pepper, cumin, oregano, chili powder, cayenne pepper
Fresh cilantro

Directions

Drain the beans and corn. Dice the onion and mince garlic.
Lay chicken breasts out to the bottom of the slow cooker. Season, to taste.
Add in onion, garlic, beans, corn, green chilies, chicken broth and chopped cilantro. Mix well.
Cook on high for 3-4 hours (low for 8 hours).
Pull out chicken and shred.

Mix in half and half and cream cheese. Put the chicken back in.

Cook on high for additional 15 min.

Once the soup thickens a little, it is ready to be served!

Chicken Taco Soup Serving 6

Prep Time: 15 min Cook Time: 8 hrs

Ingredients

1 lbs chicken breasts
1 cup mild salsa
1 can black beans (15 oz)
1 can pinto beans (15 oz)
1 can corn kernels (15oz)
1 can diced tomatoes
2 cups chicken broth
3 tbsp taco seasoning
Taco toppings (sour cream, avocado, tortilla chips or cheese)

Directions

Drain the beans and corn. Transfer to the slow cooker. Add in salsa, broth, tomatoes and taco seasoning. Stir

well. Place chicken breasts in and make sure they sink in.
Cook on low for 6 hours.
Pull out chicken and shred.
Serve with your favorite taco toppings!

Chicken Potato Soup Serving 6

Prep Time: 15 min Cook Time: 8 hrs

Ingredients

1 ½ lbs chicken breasts
3 lbs russet potatoes
4 bacon slices
1 onion
8 cups chicken broth
3 carrots
4 celery stalks
3 garlic cloves
Salt, pepper, dried thyme
Fresh parsley

Directions

Dice onion, celery, carrots and mince garlic. Peel and slice potatoes.

Cut up bacon in smaller slices, cook in the pan on the stove top. Add in onions and garlic. Sauté until onion softens. Transfer the mix in the slow cooker.

Lay chicken down on the onion mix, load in potatoes, carrots, celery and broth. Season, to taste.

Cook on high for 8 hours. Stir every hour, cook until potatoes are soft. Check the chicken, if it is done before potatoes, pull it out and shred (don't put it back in until potatoes are done!).

Mix the soup and dump the chicken back in.

Serve with some fresh chopped parsley or cheese (or both!) on top!

Beef and Barley Soup Serving 4

Prep Time: 15 min Cook Time: 9 hrs

Ingredients

1 lbs stew meat
½ cup barley
1 onion
2 carrots
2 celery stalks
2 garlic cloves
2 potatoes
4 cup beef broth
1 can crushed tomatoes (28 oz)
2 tbsp olive oil
Oregano, basil, thyme, parsley, montreal steak seasoning, salt, pepper
1 tbsp sugar
1 tbsp Worcestershire sauce

Directions

Slice carrots and celery; dice onion and mince garlic. Peel and cube potatoes.

In the pan on the stove top brown up the meat and transfer to the slow cooker.

Add in carrots, celery, onion, tomatoes, potatoes and garlic. Pour in the broth. Season, to taste. Add in Worcestershire sauce and sugar.

Cook on low for 8 hours.

Stir in barley and cook for another hour.

Serve hot!

Vegetable Beef Soup Serving 4

Prep Time: 15 min Cook Time: 8 hrs

Ingredients

1 ½ lbs stew meat
Bag of frozen vegetable mix (24 oz)
4 cup diced potatoes
1 onion
1 can diced tomatoes
1 can great nothern beans
32 oz beef broth
1 tbsp oil
2 bay leaves
Garlic powder, salt, pepper

Directions

Cube the meat and brown up in the pan with oil. Season with salt and pepper, to taste. Transfer to the slow cooker.

Dice the onion.

Load the slow cooker with onion, veggie mix, potatoes, tomatoes (with the juice from the can), beans (drained!!). Pour in the broth. Drop in the bay leaves and season, to taste. Stir well.

Cook on high for 4-5 hours (low for 8-10).

Once the potatoes are soft, pull out the bay leaves and serve!

www.ingramcontent.com/pod-product-compliance
Lightning Source LLC
Chambersburg PA
CBHW071436070526
44578CB00001B/104